Tokin' Women
A 4000-Year Herstory

By
Nola Evangelista

Evangelista Sista Press

Copyright 2016 Ellen Komp & Evangelista Sista Publishing

Cover art: *Women of Algiers,* Eugène Delacroix

[Paperback book]
ISBN 978-1-58790-352-6
ISBN 1-58790-352-0

[E-Book]
ISBN 978-1-58790-353-3
ISBN 1-58790-353-9

Library of Congress Catalog Number
2016934895

All rights reserved.

Evangelista Sista Publishing
An imprint of Regent Press
www.RegentPress.net

FOREWORD

It has long been speculated that the domination of women in our culture has coincided with the suppression of healing herbs and plant allies like cannabis that ancient medicine women utilized. To bring some balance back to the equation, this book presents profiles of over 50 females connected to cannabis through the ages, starting with ancient goddesses right up to the film goddesses of today.

The recent surge of marijuana's popularity has largely been enjoyed by men, who make up most of the readership of magazines like *High Times* as well as the ranks of activist groups like NORML and the growing marijuana industry. But that is rapidly changing, as women are organizing themselves in groups of their own, and bringing back the spirit of the goddess along with the freedom to enjoy her.

These women don't tend to look, talk or think like the pervasive male stoner stereotype. For example, many mothers in the Phoenix area surveyed by the website Chikii.com admitted in 2007 that they use marijuana as a relaxant. "These were middle to upper-middle class women, professional women, mommies," said surveyor Shay Pausa. "We had some that were members of the PTA and one school teacher even reported."

According to a 2011 *Time* magazine article, researchers found that men who were given material to read suggesting that marijuana damages the brain performed worse on cognitive tests afterwards than men who didn't. However, women actually scored better on tests of verbal skills and memory than women who weren't given the negative information. "I think that the stoner identity reads differently to women," said researcher Mitch Earleywine. "They were like, 'I'll show you!'"

Or maybe there's a chemical reason. Estrogen might help protect women from some of the learning and memory issues caused by the main active ingredient in marijuana, Louisiana State University researchers predicted, based on a 2009 study on rats. (The protection did not seem to apply, however, if the female rats were exposed to cannabis during the time period equivalent to human adolescence.)

Women, of course, are often the caregivers in our society, either as mothers or as daughters and sisters. This can give us a more compassionate view towards the medical benefits of cannabis, as well as righteous indignation about the laws that prevent relief in our loved ones. "When my mother-in-law was in the final, harrowing throes of pancreatic cancer, she had only one good day, and that was the day she smoked pot," wrote Marie Myung-Ok Lee in the *New York Times*. "We were of course raring to make the magic happen again, but it never did. The pot just frightened her too much."

Mavis Becker, a Vancouverite in her 60s, told CTV in 2007 that she has a lot of stress caring for her 93-year-old father who suffers from dementia. When she gets wound up, Mavis rolls herself a joint. "I hope my grandchildren will be willing to roll a doobie for me if my arthritis gets too bad," she said.

Longtime cannabis user Ruth Bergner outed herself in her 2005 autobiography, *I Smoke Pot with My Family: Speaking Up at 85*. "I don't have to apologize for my hearing aids or my blood pressure medication, why should I have to apologize for pot, my emotional vitamin?" asks Bergner. "With just one puff, I am instantly more open, communicative, loving and forgiving... I believe that, when used wisely, this substance supports us in learning to be more loving and emotionally sound human beings," Bergner said.

Proof of marijuana's healthful properties can be found in the story of Fulla Nayak, the world's oldest woman when she died in at the age of 125 in 2006. Nayak attributed her longevity to her daily use of marijuana.

Yet women have been targeted by the war on marijuana, as have men.

The first known raids against marijuana gardens in the US, which took place in California in 1914, included a raid on the home of Mrs. Marie Yabona of Los Angeles, the aunt of boxer Joe Rivers. The *LA Times* reported on Sept. 3, 1914, "Among the Mexican users of the drug, it is believed that those who smoke it have the power of prophecy and divination. Mexican women use it to locate deserting husbands, believing that in the fantasies induced by the drug the missing husband can be seen." For many years, I never met a person of Mexican descent who *didn't* tell me that their grandmother used marijuana for her arthritis, or for the aches and pains of getting older.

Women are often excluded from medical studies, due to the cyclic nature of our hormones and the fact that pregnancy can interfere with studies. We need to demand more research not only into the use of marijuana during pregnancy and breastfeeding, but also for PMS and cancer, particularly breast cancer. PMS is joked about, but it's actually quite serious: The suicide rate among menstruating women is significantly higher during PMS than at other times in their cycle, so we're talking life and death. The US government has known since the 1970s that cannabis has anti-tumor effects, and recent studies confirm it specifically targets breast cancer cells.

As we celebrate our "herstory," let's also join together in envisioning and working towards a new day where science rather than prejudice, and acceptance rather than repression, guides our policy. I hope this book will enlighten women and men as we move past our enforced ignorance into a wiser world that focuses on our very real problems (climate change, economic injustice, hunger and disease) instead of scapegoating people who choose a "different" means of relaxation or healing. As the pages of this book demonstrate, our herstory is long and deep, and we must hold our heads high and say, "Enough!"

—Nola Evangelista, April 2016

Photo: British Museum

The goddess Ishtar, whose aromatic herb was qunnabu (cannabis) (2300 B.C.E.)

In ancient Sumeria, "Ishtar was held in high esteem as a heavenly monarch," writes Jeanne Achterberg in *Woman as Healer*. "Her temples have been found at virtually every level of excavation." The Ishtar Gate to the inner city of Babylon was one of the ancient wonders of the world.

Also called the Queen of Heaven, Ishtar was a compassionate, healing deity. Her medicine kit likely included plant allies: A clay pot probably used for distillation of plant essences into medicines was found at a Sumerian grave site circa 5500 B.C.E. The herb called Sim.Ishara, meaning "aromatic of the Goddess Ishtar," is the Akkadian qunnabu, or "cannabis," writes Assyriologist Erica Reiner.

As the land of Sumer became a perpetual battlefield, Ishtar became the goddess of war and destiny, and became more sexualized, even as women were restricted from education and the healing arts. In mankind's first written story, *The Epic of Gilgamesh* (circa 2000 B.C.E), the cruel king Gilgamesh calls Ishtar a predatory and promiscuous woman, and rebukes her advances, just before taking off with his buddy Enkidu to chop down the great cedar forest. Gilgamesh's repudiation of Ishtar, some scholars say, signifies a rejection of goddess worship in favor of patriarchy in ancient times.

In ancient Babylon, around the spring solstice, people celebrated the resurrection of their god Tammuz, who was brought back from the underworld by his mother/wife Ishtar (pronounced "Easter" in most Semitic dialects). Flowers, painted eggs, and rabbits were the symbols of the holiday then, as now.

Thus the goddess Ishtar resurrects every spring at Easter time, by way of the German goddess Ostara, "the divinity of the radiant dawn," doubtlessly a reincarnation of Ishtar, who the Babylonians called "the morning star" and "the perfect light." The biblical heroine Esther is also named for Ishtar.

Princess Ukok

buried with a container of cannabis (1500 B.C.E.)

Scientist Natalia Polosmak discovered the remains of an elaborately tattooed mummy known as 'Princess Ukok' high in the Altai Mountains in 1993. Buried with her were six horses, saddled and bridled, her spiritual escorts to the next world and a symbol of her evident status—perhaps as a revered folk tale narrator, a healer, or a holy woman rather than an ice princess. She was possibly a high priestess of the Pazyryk people, who were closely related to the Scythians, a tribe that inhaled cannabis smoke ritually, as described by the Greek historian Herodotus in 440 B.C.E.

Along with a meal of sheep and horse meat and ornaments made from felt, wood, bronze and gold, the tomb contained a small container of cannabis, say some accounts.

Now a team of Russian scientists say MRI technology has found evidence of breast cancer, the bone infection osteomyelitis, and injuries consistent with a fall—perhaps from a horse—in the Ice Princess. Polosmak wrote in a recent issue of the journal *Science First Hand*: "It is likely that for this sick woman, the regular inhalation of cannabis smoke was a necessity."

A California company calling itself Altai Brands in Princess Ukok's honor manufactures artisanal cannabis-infused edibles. "Her story is an inspiration to re-educate and re-contextualize the meaning of cannabis use in our modern culture," says their website.

There is also archeological evidence that ancient women used cannabis as an aide to childbirth. A study in 1992 found THC on the stomach of a young woman giving birth in a Judean cave in 1700 B.C.E. Cannabinoid residues were also found in a nearby glass vessel used to burn cannabis so that its smoke could be inhaled. (Zlas, 1993).

Photo: Luxor Temple

The Egyptian goddess Seshat,
"She of Seven Points"
(1250 B.C.E.)

Seshat (also spelled Safkhet, Sesat, Seshet, Sesheta, and Seshata) was the ancient Egyptian goddess of mathematics, creative thought, knowledge, books and writing. (Her name means "she who is the scribe.") Sister to Bast and daughter/sister/wife to Thoth or the moon god Djehuti, the Egyptians believed that she invented writing, while Thoth or Djehuti taught writing to mankind.

Often depicted in coronation ceremonies wearing a leopard-skin garment, Seshat's emblem is a seven-pointed leaf in her headdress that looks much like hemp. Pharaoh Tuthmosis III (1479-1425 B.C.E.) called her Sefket-Abwy (She of Seven Points).

It was Seshat who the Pharaoh consulted as to the orientation and structure of temples to be built. Hemp rope was used in the "stretching the cord" ceremonies conducted before building. It is perhaps hemp's psychoactive effect that is acknowledged in the saying, "Seshat opens the door of heaven for you."

Hemp fibers were found in the tomb of Amenphis IV ca. 1350 B.C.E. and cannabis pollen was found inside the mummy of Ramses II, who died ca. 1213 B.C.E. Cannabis is mentioned as a medication as far back as 1700 B.C.E. in Egypt, possibly copying earlier texts that date back to 3100 B.C.E. Seshat was associated with Isis in the Late period, and was scribe to Hathsheput, the female Pharaoh of the 18th dynasty. The Greeks demoted the goddess to a muse, and Plato gives over to Thoth the invention of arithmetic and letters.

Researcher Chris Bennett and others connect Ishtar with Ishara, the prototypical Semitic goddess of love and medicine dating back to the third milennium B.C.E. "Ishara" is the Hittite word for "treaty, binding promise" and so could connect with hempen rope. "Ishtar was often depicted as a bundle of reeds, known as the 'knot of Ishtar,'" writes Bennett in *Cannabis and the Soma Solution*.)

Queen of Sheba

Bringer of Spices

(950 B.C.E.)

The biblical Queen of Sheba, who also appears in the Quran and is claimed by the Ethiopians as theirs, famously brought gold and spices to King Solomon, whose temple was dedicated "for the burning of the incense of sweet spices before him" (2 Chronicles 2:4)

Some archaeologists think she was a Sabaean from the Semitic civilization of Saba (1200 B.C.E–275 A.D.) in Southern Arabia, now Yemen. Two ancient Yemeni peoples, the Mineans and the Sabaeans, were involved in the spice trade, and among the names of incense inscribed on South Arabian incense burners is *Qlm* which "identifies with calamus, also known as scented reed, described by Pliny as having 'a specially fine scent which attracts people even from a long way off,'" (*Queen of Sheba: Treasures from Ancient Yemen*, St. John Simpson, ed.).

The inscription on a wooden sarcophagus dated 264 BC from Egypt shows it contained the body of a Minaean trader who "imported myrrh and calamus for the temples of the gods of Egypt." Anthropologist Sula Benet argued that in the earliest Greek translations of the Old Testament, "cannabis" was erroneously translated as "calamus."

Islamic versions of the legend of the Queen of Sheba (aka Bilqis) have a strange plot in which Solomon polishes the palace floor so that he can see the Queen's legs, which were reputed to be the legs of a donkey. A female demon famous for having the legs of a donkey is mentioned in Aristophanes' comedy *The Frogs* (see p. 13).

The Testament of Solomon says that a donkey-legged woman took part in the construction of the temple of Jerusalem by producing hempen ropes. This role is similar to that of the ancient Egyptian goddess Seshat, who was scribe to Hathsheput (see p. 8). Some think that The Queen of Sheba was Hathsepsut herself, or one of her descendants. Sheba means "star" or "seven," a number associated with Seshat. Asterion, meaning star, was one of the ancient Greek names for cannabis, and the asterion plant was offered to the goddess Hera (Rigoglioso).

Photo: The Louvre Museum

Helen of Troy, purveyor of Nepenthe

(900 B.C.E.)

Homer's *The Odyssey* (900 B.C.E) speaks of nepenthe, Helen's drug of forgetting one's sorrow, which she is said to have obtained from an Egyptian queen named Polydamna or Polymnestes, and brought it from Thebes. Historian Diodorus wrote in 1814, "in that city, to this day, women use this medicine with good success."

Helen, whose face launched the thousand ships of the Trojan war, serves nepenthe mixed in wine to Telemachus, who is searching for his missing father Odysseus. Scholars speculate the drug was a mixture of opium, mandrake, henbane, belladonna and hashish.

Elsewhere in the Greek epic, wandering warriors visit the Land of the Lotus Eaters, where they again forget their woes, and the goddess Circe's magic herbs turn the men into swine (with the exception of Odysseus, who is protected by the holy 'moly' herb and coached by Circe on his trip to the underworld). In Homer, heroes do not die but are sent to the heavenly and peaceful Elysian fields.

In 440 B.C.E the historian Herodotus observed Scythians using cannabis ritualistically, around the time Greek playwrights Aristophanes and Orestes wrote about the Eleusinian mysteries, the yearly rituals that were the Burning Man of their day. *The Frogs* by Aristophanes (405 B.C.E.) involves the sybaritic Dionysus as the new god of Eleusis. Some scholars think the play focuses on the exiled general Alcibiades, who stole the Eleusinian sacrament *kykeon* from the temple of the grain goddess Demeter, and started partying with it at orgies at his home.

In 392 AD, the Romans outlawed Eleusis and the Delphic oracle, a series of women who some (e.g. Marguerite Rigoglioso) speculate were inhaling gases or cannabis. In *The Aeneid*, Roman writer Virgil makes the Elysian fields a part of Hades. Greek knowledge passed into the Islamic world, where scholars kept it alive until the Western universities rediscovered it between the 10th and 12th centuries.

Photo: *Jezebel and Ahab Met by Elijah* by Frederic Leighton

Princess Jezebel,

devotee of Bel

(900 B.C.E.)

Jezebel was a 9th century Phoenician princess who married Ahab the prince of Israel, but maintained her loyalty to the god Bel, a descendant of Belili, the Sumerian White Goddess. Jeze-bel means "where is Bel."

Throughout the Old Testament, prophet after prophet warns the children of Israel that God will bring misery upon them unless they cease to burn incense to worship Baal or Bel, and his consort Ashtoreth, the Biblical name for the ancient Babylonian goddess Ishtar (see p. 4). Some scholars think that the "burnt offerings" made to Ashtoreth and Baal/Bel were cannabis, mistranslated as "calamus" from *kaneh bosm* (sweet or good cane) in scripture.

The prophet Jeremiah portends disaster for Jerusalem because of all the incense burning and Bal worshiping going on. Elijah outwits followers of Bel on Mount Carmel; among them Jezebel, who had brought 850 worshipers of Bel to Israel and had Naboth killed so that Ahab could use his vineyard as an herb garden.

Bel eventually became Jupiter in Roman myth. Baal was depicted, in some regions, as a horned god, and his horns were adopted for the Christian image of the Devil. Elijah turns up again as the name of a prophet in *Moby Dick* who issues an unheeded warning against the book's fanatical Captain Ahab. In the book, the South Sea islander Queequeg, who smokes a tomahawk/pipe, is told to "spurn the idol Bel, and the hideous dragon." Ahab turns out to be a Zoroastrian, who worships the Queen of Heaven.

To this day "a Jezebel" is a term applied to a vain, fallen woman not to be trusted: It was the name of a Bette Davis movie where she betrays her fiancé by wearing a red dress instead of a white one. But the name has now been reclaimed by a hip website for women, Jezebel.com.

The goddess Parvati with her consort, Lord Shiva (400 B.C.E.)

Legend has it that the goddess Parvati, wife of the Hindu god Lord Shiva, brought cannabis to humankind.

It seems Shiva was busy frolicking on the mountaintops with various nymphs when Parvati, left alone at home, discovered a cannabis plant growing in her garden. When Shiva returned to her, Parvati put some of the plant into a pipe for him to smoke. He did, and thereafter the two invented tantric yoga and saved their marriage.

Rather like the Adam and Eve story, here it is the woman who discovers the magical plant (which is "forbidden" in the Bible, what Timothy Leary called "the first controlled substance").

Parvati is the Hindu mother goddess of love, fertility and devotion. Along with Lakshmi (goddess of wealth and prosperity) and Saraswati (goddess of knowledge and learning) she forms the Trinity of Hindu goddesses. Two of her forms are Durga (Goddess beyond reach) and Kali (Goddess of Destruction). She is the mother of Ganesh.

To this day, worshipers in India drink bhang (cannabis milk) during the Shivratri Festival, celebrating the marriage of Shiva and Parvati. Women in particular practice devotions during this time.

Parvati is believed to be sister to the Goddess Ganga, the personification of the sacred river Ganges and the term for cannabis leaves and flowers that are smoked. Bhang and Ganga are said to reside side by side on Shiva's head, while he dances on the body of a dwarf who embodies indifference, ignorance and laziness.

Another interpretation of these ancient myths is that the cannabis plant is another form of Parvati.

18 Tokin' Women: A 4000-Year Herstory

Photo: www.wayofinfiniteharmony.org / Sponsored by Green Rush Consulting

Goddess Magu
"The Hemp Maiden"

Magu is a Taoist xian ("inspired sage," "ecstatic") whose name means Hemp Maiden or Goddess.

Magu's name combines the Chinese character MA—which derives from a Zhou Dynasty ideograph showing plants drying in a shed—with GU, a kinship term for a woman also used in religious titles like Priestess. It's been proposed that the name is related to the Old Persian word "magus" (magician, magi).

Magu is called Mago in Korea and Mako in Japan, where a saying "Magu scratches the itch" hearkens to her long fingernails. Several early folktales from Sichuan province associate Magu with caves, and one describes a shaman who invoked her. She is said to have ascended to immortality at Magu Shan ("Magu Mountain") in Nancheng. A second Magu Mountain is located in Jianchang county.

Magu was also goddess of Shandong's sacred Mount Tai, where cannabis "was supposed to be gathered on the seventh day of the seventh month," wrote Joseph Needham in *Science and Civilization in China* (1959). Needham wrote, "There is much reason for thinking that the ancient Taoists experimented systematically with hallucinogenic smokes…at all events the incense-burner remained the centre of changes and transformations…."The (ca. 570 B.C.E.) Daoist encyclopedia records that cannabis was added into ritual censers.

Magu is often depicted flying on a crane, riding a deer or holding peaches or wine (symbols of longevity). She is associated with the elixir of life and is the protector of females. Before becoming immortal she freed slaves who were working for her evil father. She is often pictured on birthday cards in China, where cannabis has been continuously cultivated since Neolithic times. Magu's harvest festival (the seventh day of the seventh lunar month) celebrates the time "When the World Was Green."

Photo: Miniatur aus dem Rupertsberger Codex des Liber Scivias

Hildegarde von Bingen
"The Visionary"

The Dark Ages began to enlighten up when German visionary abbess Hildegarde von Bingen mentions using hemp as an herbal medication in the 11th century, around the same time the Syrian Old Man of the Mountain and his Hashishin sect began to prove so troublesome to the Crusaders, and centuries before Rabelais extolled the virtues of Pantagruelion in his epic writings.

Depicted here writing down her visions, Hildegarde read many ancient texts and corresponded with all the top leaders of her day, from popes to emperors. She left one of the largest bodies of letters to survive from the Middle Ages (nearly 400) along with many sermons she gave and musical compositions she wrote, three volumes on theology, and two volumes on natural medicines.

Florence Glaze notes in *Medical Writer: Behold the Human Creature* that Hildegarde is, "as a medical thinker, clearly interested in the broader universal context through which she might understand and explain the reasons for diseases, both cosmic and microcosmic, as well as revealing the means by which diseases might be vanquished."

Back in the eleventh century, women used it to treat swollen breasts. The Old English Herbarium described the process as follows: "Rub [the herb] with fat, lay it to the breast, it will disperse the swelling." Documents show the same method was used in nineteenth-century Germany and Austria, where cannabis was "laid on the painful breasts of women who have given birth."

Medieval herbalists recommended "hempe" against "nodes and wennes and other hard tumors." In the 1970s, lungs of mice were injected with cancer cells and cannabinoids; the size of tumors was reduced by 25-82% depending on dose and duration of treatment. Other studies have found similar results. A recent study from Harvard University researchers found that THC "seems to have a suppressive effect on certain lines of cancer cells" by curbing epidermal growth factor (EPF).

Photo: The Louvre Museum

"Women of Algiers"
Eugene Delacroix

1834

"In Victorian fiction only really dissolute women smoke. Yet in harem literature smoking is domesticated and feminised. Indeed quite a few travelers took to smoking. Mary Eliza Rogers herself, Elisabeth Finn, Lucy Stanhope and Isabel Burton smoked. And Mrs. Bird Bishop and Harriet Martineau, these two paragons of propriety, became quite addicted to the *chibouque*." —Billie Melman, *Women's Orients*

Lady Lucy Stanhope refused to wear a veil while traveling in the East in the mid-1800s, choosing instead the garb of a Turkish male: robe, turban and slippers. Isabel Burton, the wife of explorer Sir Richard Burton who translated the *Arabian Nights* and other key Eastern texts into English, was herself an author. Martineau, often called the first female sociologist, was Comte's first translator into English and a novelist and journalist who published *Eastern Life, Present and Past* in 1848. She wrote of a visit to a harem:

"Almost everybody was puffing away at a chibouque or a nargeeleh, and the place was one cloud of smoke. The poor Jewesses were obliged to decline joining us; for it happened to be Saturday: they must not smoke on the Sabbath. They were naturally much pitied: and some of the young wives did what was possible for them. Drawing a long breath of smoke, they puffed it forth in the faces of the Jewesses, who opened mouth and nostrils eagerly to receive it. Thus the Sabbath observed, to shouts of laughter."

Rogers, who traveled with her diplomat husband in Palestine and Syria, wrote in her book *Domestic Life in Palestine* (1862) of taking a meal at a harem, after which chibouques and narghiles were given to the elderly women first. "After Helweh had smoked for a few minutes, she inclined her head gracefully, placed one hand on her bosom, touched her forehead with the pliant tube, and then handed it to the lady sitting next to her, who happened to be the second wife of her own husband, Saleh Bek. Thus it was transferred from one smoker to another, even to the handmaidens, with the words, 'May it give you pleasure.'"

Photo: George Eliot, aged 30, by Alexandre-Louis-François d'Albert-Durade

George Eliot
"The Lifted Veil"

Mary Ann Evans, who wrote epic books like *Middlemarch* and *The Mill on the Floss* under the name George Eliot in the mid 1800s, was Jane Austen with a political twist.

Apparently Englishmen and women who traveled to the East in the mid-1800s brought back hashish for domestic consumption; tinctures were also available in pharmacies for a variety of illnesses.

In "English Traits" (1856), Ralph Waldo Emerson wrote:

"The young men have a rude health which runs into peccant humors. They drink brandy like water...They stoutly carry into every nook and corner of the earth their turbulent sense; leaving no lie uncontradicted; no pretension unexamined. They chew hasheesh....and measure their own strength by the terror they cause."

By contrast, Evans's mention of hashish in *The Lifted Veil* (1859) seems rather tame: "She intoxicated me with the sense that I was necessary to her… A half-repressed word, a moment's unexpected silence, even an easy fit of petulance on our account, will serve us as hashish for a long while."

Literary critic Harold Bloom placed Eliot among the greatest Western writers of all time; *Middlemarch* has been described by Martin Amis and Julian Barnes as the greatest novel in the English language. Conservative columnist George Will put it on a list of ten things he would take to another planet, along with Susan Sarandon (p. 118).

Photo: www.ephemeralnewyork.wordpress.com

Ada Clare
"Queen of the Bohemians"

Rebel Souls: Walt Whitman and America's First Bohemians by Justin Martin describes a fascinating cast of characters who hung out at Pfaff's bar in New York City in the mid-1800s. Among them were Fitz Hugh Ludlow, author of *The Hasheesh Eater* (1857) and Ada Clare, an actress and writer crowned "Queen of the Bohemians."

Clare wrote a review of fellow boho Fitz James O'Brien's story "Mother of Pearl" in *The New York Saturday Press*, January 1860:

"The drug called hasheesh has become too well domesticated to assist in a crisis now. It is on too good terms with the digestion. Let us have some drug more awful and mystic to round off our harrowing climaxes—buckwheat for instance: it is time that the buckwheat-cake-eater should come forth and soliloquize." (In the O'Brien story she cites it is a female who takes the hasheesh, and commits murder. Clare rightly dismisses this as poppycock.)

An acolyte of Clare's, actress/poet Dora Shaw, was apparently inspired by Ludlow's writings to try hashish on July 4, 1859 with novelist/utopianist Marie Stevens Case, who recorded the event in *The New York Saturday Press* (7/16/59). Marie writes:

"Dora, who is always witty, was especially happy on this occasion, and we remained convulsed until laughter seemed the most boundless and exquisite pleasure in the world." Marie, who tripled her initial dose, then imagines she has become a sphinx made of stone and envisions entering a painting of Cleopatra, and being tended to by mummies.

Feeling as though years had passed, the women are surprised to discover that their adventures lasted only two hours, so they dress and go to watch the fireworks. "The effect of the hascheesh was still upon us a little," Marie wrote, "and the rockets seemed the most astonishing and gorgeous things in the universe."

Photo: Alcott at age 20

Louisa May Alcott

"Heaven bless hashish, if its dreams end like this."

The woman best known as the author of *Little Women* started to contribute to her family's income at the age of 15, taking various positions including teacher, seamstress, and servant before earning an income with her pen.

In 1860, Louisa May Alcott began writing for the *Atlantic Monthly*, and she worked as a nurse in the Union Hospital at Georgetown, D.C. for six weeks in 1862-1863. Her letters home, collected as *Hospital Sketches* (1863), garnered her first critical recognition for her observations and humor. But like many other nurses, Alcott contracted typhoid fever and although she recovered, she would suffer the poisoning effects of calomel, a drug laden with mercury then used to cure typhoid, for the rest of her life.

Starting in the 1860s, the Ganja Wallah Hasheesh Candy Company made and marketed maple sugar hashish candy. In Philadelphia during the American Centennial Exposition of 1876, the Turkish exhibition included a hookah and at least one local pharmacist sold hashish.

In 1869, Alcott published "Perilous Play," a short story wherein a group of young socialites enjoys hashish bon-bons. One of the characters named Rose St. Just, who is dark like Alcott, sits reading *The Lotus Eaters*. Of taking hashish, she says, "I hoped it would make me soft and lovable, like other women. I'm tired of being a lonely statue."

A Modern Mephistopheles, the novel Alcott wrote in 1867 as *A Long Fatal Love Chase* and published anonymously in 1877, contains a much fuller description of hashish's effects. Jasper Helwyze, the book's devilish character, is an opium addict (as was Alcott, for medicinal reasons) who slowly seduces Gladys, the innocent young wife of his colleague Felix Canaris, with Eastern delights. "I feel as if I could do anything to-night," Gladys announces, and she came to them "with a swift step, an eager air, as if longing to find some outlet for the strange energy which seemed to thrill every nerve and set her heart beating audibly."

Crop of a photograph taken by MediaJet of a portrait; Wikipedia Creative Commons

"It is one of the most valuable medicines."

J.R. Reynolds, physician to Queen Victoria

We don't know whether or not Queen Victoria used cannabis. We do however know that Sir John Russell Reynolds, who served a thirty-seven year tenure as one of Victoria's personal physicians, wrote that he found cannabis useful for treating menstrual cramps, migraine, neuralgia, epileptic convulsions, and senile insomnia. Reynolds wrote a scientific review of cannabis in 1890 that noted, "When pure and administered carefully, it is one of the most valuable medicines we possess."

Victoria was adventurous enounght to be an early user of chloroform as anaesthesia during childbirth, writing in her diary in 1853, "Dr. Snow [the inventor of the chloroform inhaler] gave that blessed chloroform and the effect was soothing, quieting, and delightful beyond measure."

It's been suggested that modern British royal Princess Kate ought to try cannabis to treat her hyperemesis gravidarum (HG), a debilitating ailment characterized by severe nausea and vomiting, malnutrition, and weight loss during pregnancy that afflicts 1-2% of pregnant women globally. Since cannabis is the safest and most effective anti-emetic known, it would make sense to consider it a remedy for mothers with severe morning sickness.

Some studies in rats indicate low birth weight can be a problem for cannabis-using mothers (as it can for mothers who have HG). But a marijuana and pregnancy study funded by the March of Dimes and published in the journal *Pediatrics* in 1994 found that the children of marijuana-smoking mothers in Jamaica actually did better on behavioral tests than did the children of nonsmoking mothers.

Graduate student Wei-Ni Lin Curry collected stories from women with HG who found relief with cannabis in the book *Women and Cannabis: Medicine, Science and Sociology* (Haworth Press, 2002). Curry's Taiwanese obstetrician told her that "since ancient times the Chinese have used cannabis to treat HG," and recent studies have found that only small amounts of THC cross over the placental barrier to the fetus (Dreher, *Cannabis and Pregnancy*, 1997).

Photo of Mary Todd Lincoln 1846-1847 by Nicolas H. Shepherd

Mary Todd Lincoln

"The Hemp Farmer's Daughter"

After the death of her husband and two of her three sons, Mary Todd Lincoln was sent to a sanitarium where hashish was prescribed. As with Queen Victoria, we don't know whether or not cannabis was prescribed for the former first lady.

Mary Todd was from a prominent family of hemp farmers in Lexington, Kentucky. According to the Kentucky Office in Lexington: "Hemp was introduced at an early date [in Fayette county]. Nathan Burrowes, a county resident, invented a machine for cleaning it in 1796. The soil produced fine hemp and in 1870 the county grew 4.3 million pounds. The crop declined in the 1890s because of increased demand for tobacco and competition from imported hemp from the Philippines. In 1941, when the federal government saw a possible shortage of manila rope from the Philippines, farmers were encouraged to grow hemp once again for use in World War II. The crop declined again in 1945."

After their marriage in 1842, the Lincolns visited Lexington several times and stayed at the family home on Main street, which is open to the public today. Nearby is the Hunt-Morgan house, built in 1814 for the first millionaire west of the Alleghenies, a hemp merchant named John Wesley Hunt. Among Hunt's descendants was Confederate General John Hunt Morgan, the flamboyant leader of the guerrilla fighters known as "Morgan's Raiders."

On November 5, 1849, President Lincoln wrote a letter to Secretary of the Navy William B. Preston, recommending Mary Todd's uncle, Dr. John T. Parker, for the Hemp Agency of Kentucky.

Rumors that Abraham Lincoln wrote a letter saying he liked to smoke a hemp pipe and play his harmonica after dinner on his porch are also unconfirmed, although Lincoln did play the harmonica and his Secretary of State John Hay wrote about trying hashish in college.

Helena Blavatsky

"Hashish multiplies one's life a thousandfold."

The famed 19th century Russian born mystic, world traveler, feminist, Theosophical Society co-founder, and author of occult classics *Isis Unveiled* and *The Secret Doctrine*, Helena Petrova Blavatsky is also reputed to have been a user of cannabis.

"She wrote, sometimes under the influence of hashish, several books filled with esoteric lore, which owed a great deal to Hindu and Buddhist systems of thought, and brought to public awareness in the West such concepts as karma, prana, kundalini, yoga and reincarnation," said Benjamin Walker in *Tantrism: Its Secret Principles and Practices*.

A.L. Rawson, a longtime friend of Blavatsky who she praises in *Isis Unveiled*, wrote that "she had tried hasheesh in Cairo with success, and she again indulged in it in this city under the care of myself and Dr. Edward Sutton Smith, who had had a large experience with the drug among his patients at Mount Lebanon, Syria."

Rawson wrote that Blavatsky said:

"Hasheesh multiplies one's life a thousandfold. My experiences are as real as if they were ordinary events of actual life. Ah! I have the explanation. It is a recollection of my former existences, my previous incarnations. It is a wonderful drug and it clears up profound mystery."

The modern-day Theosophical society minimizes the effect hashish may have had on Blavatsky, pointing to some negative comments she made about it later in life when she was ill.

Photo: Library of Congress, George Grantham Bain Collection

Maud Gonne

"Thank you for the dream drug."

"I had never thought to see in a living woman so great beauty. It belonged to famous pictures, to some legendary past," is how William Butler Yeats described the young Maud Gonne. Yeats proposed marriage several times to Gonne, and the two remained lifelong friends and compatriots in the Irish nationalist cause despite her refusals.

The statuesque (six-foot-tall) beauty attracted the attention of the Prince of Wales at her coming-out party and tried her hand at acting until she discovered she had an inheritance. After her political awakening, she traveled Europe winning support for the Irish cause. Nancy Cardozo wrote in *Lucky Eyes and a High Heart, The Life of Maud Gonne,* "She wrung tears from cynical politicians and sous from the pockets of students who adopted the eloquent young beauty and carried her off to speak to Republican and Catholic societies in the provinces....A thousand people gave her a standing ovation in Bordeaux."

Yeats took Gonne to a meeting of the Theosophical Society and introduced her to Madame Blavatsky (p. 34), near the end of her life. Together Gonne and Yeats took hashish in Paris in 1894 in "an attempt to make themselves telepathic." Later they experimented with mescal given to Yeats by Havelock Ellis.

"I have to thank you for the dream drug which I have not tried as yet being very busy & having need of all my energy & activity for the moment but I mean to try it soon," Gonne wrote Yeats in April or May 1897. She was probably referring to hashish or mescal.

Gonne's image was used in an ad for Vin Mariani, the coca-laced wine that had many famous enthusiasts. She said of it, "Your coca-wine by fortifying my voice will allow me make my beloved country better known." She used chloroform for insomnia, and the story goes that, substituting cannabis for her insomnia instead, had awoken one night to find herself apparently transported to the bedside of her sister.

Photo: Isabelle Eberhardt in the Sahel desert, circa 1900

Isabelle Eberhardt

"A Feminine Rimbaud"

The illegitimate daughter of a Russian noblewoman and her children's anarchistic tutor, Isabelle Eberhardt was raised to be an independent thinker and her short but eventful life proved she was. At the age of 20, she left France for Algeria with her mother, who died suddenly six months later. Despondent, Isabelle turned to drink (and quite likely kif) and befriended Muslim students who revolted against French colonialism. She embraced Islam and picked up a sword to join a revolt.

Sometimes dressed as a man, Eberhardt explored the region, sending dispatches in the form of crystalline short stories like "The Seduced," a heartbreaking tale of a young Arab seduced into joining the army who returns to see his family's land usurped. Like Gertrude Bell (p. 40), she spied at times, and like explorer Richard Francis Burton she joined the secret Sufi brotherhood Qadiriyya. In 1901, she married Slimane Ehnni, an Algerian soldier. She died at the age of 27 when a flash flood collapsed the roof of a clay house where she and Ehnni were staying.

Eberhardt's novel *The Vagabond* was published after her death; her short story collection *The Oblivion Seekers* was translated into English by Paul Bowles. A book of her stories and reviews of her work, *Departures*, was published in 1994 by City Lights (San Francisco).

One reviewer wrote, "She plays with shadows and with light, masculine and feminine, debauchery and religion....Her immoderate love of absinthe, kif, and often-dangerous liaisons, frequently evokes the image of a feminine Rimbaud" (www.lafeuillecharbinoise.com). A European acquaintance said of her, "She drank more than a Legionnaire, smoked more kif than a hashish addict, and made love for the love of making love." (Source: *Isabelle: The Life of Isabelle Eberhardt* by Annette Kobak.)

Tokin' Woman Patti Smith (p. 100) mentions reading Eberhardt in her bestselling book *Just Kids* and her new book *M Train*.

Photographic Archive, Department of Archaeology, University of Newcastle upon Tyne

Gertrude Bell
"Queen of the Desert"

In 1914, Gertrude Bell wrote a letter recounting this legend she heard during her travels in Arab lands:

There were three men, one drank arak [a distilled alcoholic drink], the other wine, and the third hashish. And when they rose to go out of the house they looked at the door. And the Father of arak said, "It is great as the door of a khan, we can never open it." The Father of wine said, "It is open and the flood of a river is flowing through, we cannot pass." But the Father of hashish said, "Then we must climb the wall. And he climbed the wall and dropped into the street."

Bell was a mountaineer and a self-styled diplomat, later a spy, who was instrumental in drawing the current borders of Iraq and establishing the Iraq Museum in Baghdad. The 1997 film *The English Patient* makes a reference to a Bell map (incorrectly identifying her as a man).

A spirited and brilliant child whose grandfather was a railroad magnate, Bell earned a college degree in history with honors in only two years and became a serious student of Arabic. She fell in love with a young officer who read her Hafiz, the Sufi poet, but her parents refused to allow them to marry. She never married, but she did publish a translation of Hafiz.

Bell went on many adventurous quests through Arabia, meeting sheiks who treated her like a visiting queen. *Gertrude Bell: Queen of the Desert, Shaper of Nations* by Georgina Howell says of Bell, "Her Arabic had become good enough for her to discuss desert politics with notables she met long the way. She began to take her turn with the *narghileh* that was passed around as they talked, the bubble-pipe in which tobacco, marijuana, or opium was smoked. She did not enjoy it at first, as she was at pains to tell her parents, but gradually acquired the habit."

Nicole Kidman portrays Bell in the movie "Queen of the Desert," due for release in late 2015.

SFMoMA: The Steins Collect Exhibition

Marie Laurençin
"Les Invités" 1908

An illegitimate child, Marie Laurençin was born in Paris in 1883 to a Creole mother who worked as a seamstress. She began her career as a porcelain painter at the Sèvres factory and attended the Académie Humbert where she met Georges Braque. She soon became part of the avant garde artist set in Paris.

In 1907 Laurençin exhibited her paintings at the Salon des Indépendants and was introduced to Apollinaire. The two artists began an affair that lasted until 1913, and she has also been linked with Picasso and with other women. Rodin called her "a woman who is neither futurist nor cubist. She knows what gracefulness is; it is serpentine." Picasso purchased her painting *La Songeuse* (1911) and kept it all his life.

Max Ernst painted her portrait, as did Cocteau. In 1912, Laurençin and two other women fought off angry viewers of the controversial Cubist House with their umbrellas. Gertrude Stein (p. 44) purchased Laurençin's *Les Invités* (shown), the painter's first sale. It is a record of an infamous 1908 dinner party where hashish pills were taken at Azon's restaurant in Paris. Laurençin's self portrait is at upper left, with knowing eyes, flanked by Picasso and Apollinaire. Fernande Oliver, Picasso's mistress, is at bottom right.

The following year, Laurençin painted *Un Réunion a la Campagne* (A Reunion in the Country), where she is depicted reclining as a hostess would, along with the three from *Les Invités* and others. Thus Laurençin is possibly the first person to paint a pot party (or two). In the first portrait she is the most fully realized image, and is bringing a flower: was she the instigator for the hashish taking who invited the others? She may have been a lover of Princess Violette Murat (p. 46), who could have supplied her.

Laurençin was named chevalier of the Légion d'honneur in 1937 and in 1983, the Marie Laurençin Museum in Nagano-Ken, Japan was inaugurated to celebrate the centenary of her birth.

Photo: www.theredlist.fr

"I love you Alice B. Toklas"

The hostesses with the most-est who brought expatriate writers and artists together at their Parisian salon, Gertrude Stein and Alice B. Toklas were, in essence, gay married long before it was cool.

Much has been made of Toklas and her hashish fudge, a recipe for which appears in *The Alice B. Toklas Cookbook*, first published in 1954. But when Toklas's American publisher objected to the "illegal" recipe, she feared many would assume Stein's writing happened while under the influence (which certainly seems possible, if you read it). Toklas disavowed knowledge of the recipe, which was contributed by the author Brion Gysin.

It's possible that Stein and Toklas were more conduits for a younger generation of partakers, like Gysin and his friend Paul Bowles, who lived with Stein and Toklas for a time. The Lost Generation was, after all, mostly lost in liquor.

However an interesting character by the name of Jenny Reefer appears in "The Mother of Us All," a 1947 opera about the life and career of suffragette Susan B. Anthony for which Stein wrote the libretto. Reefer is described as "a mezzo-soprano; a comical feminist, outspoken and opinionated." Sounds like a pothead to me.

The 1968 film *I Love You Alice B. Toklas* won Leigh Taylor-Young a Golden Globe nomination for her luminous performance as a hippie chick who turns Peter Sellers on to pot brownies, a year before *Easy Rider* broke open pot smoking on film.

In a 1969 episode of the TV show *Bewitched*, Endora (Agnes Moorehead) is offered cookies by Darrin's (straight) mother. "They're not by chance from an Alice B. Toklas recipe?" Endora asks. When told they were not, "Then I think I'll pass," is her answer.

Photo by Berenice Abbott, Parasol Press

Princess Violette Murat

"A Very High Liver"

In his memoir *Chiaroscuro* (1952), Welch painter and "King of the Bohemians" Augustus John described a 1920s dinner party at the home of photographer Curtis Moffatt, "a bit of a sybarite" who was married to poet Iris Tree (p. 48):

"When he lived in Hampstead, Curtis used to give small parties at which sardines and wine were consumed—and sometimes hashish. I had already tried smoking this celebrated drug without the slightest result. It was Princess Murat who converted me. She contributed several pots of the substance in the form of a compôte or jam. A teaspoonful was taken at intervals. Having helped myself to the first dose I had almost forgotten it when, catching the eye of Iris Tree across the dinner table, we were both simultaneously seized with uncontrollable laughter about nothing at all."

Violette Ney D'Elchingen was a Bonaparte princess born September 9, 1878. Granddaughter of Napoleon's marshal Michael Ney, she was the wife of (Eugene) Joachim Murat (1875-1906), a descendant of the Joachim Murat (1767-1815) who married Caroline Bonaparte, Napoleon's sister. The painting *Grand Odalisque* by Ingres (1814), commissioned by Caroline Bonaparte Murat, depicts what looks like a hash or opium pipe in the corner.

The book *Cote D'Azur: Inventing The French Riviera* includes the following insight into the lifestyles of the rich and famous in the 1920s: "Princess Violette Murat, friends say, not only bought her opium in Toulon, but also rented a submarine in order to smoke it in peace."

Along with Tallulah Bankhead (p. 60), Murat was part of the Harlem renaissance in the 1920s. Berenice Abbott, who photographed Murat (shown), wrote of her, "A very high liver. Oh, all kinds of wonderful tales are told about her....She...knew how to make an art out of living and that's something stupendous. Anything she did became a vibrant, extraordinary event. I can remember seeing her go into a ten-cent store and buy the place out and have a fling doing it."

Photo: Iris Tree by Augustus John

Iris Tree
Poet, Actress Adventuress

You preach to me of laws, you tie my limbs
With rights and wrongs and arguments of good,
You choke my songs and fill my mouth with hymns,
You stop my heart and turn it into wood...

Thus begins Iris Tree's first book of poems, published in 1919. The daughter of famed English actor and impresario Sir Herbert Tree, Iris was a free thinker from an early age. At 17 she met her lifelong friend Augustus John, with whom she had a fit of giggles over a pot of hashish jam at a 1920s party (see p. 47).

Tree came to America to act, roamed around California, then moved back to Europe with her second husband where they were involved in the Chekhov Theatre Studio. She appears in a cameo, reading poetry as herself, in Federico Fellini's *La Dolce Vita* (1960).

Around 1940 Tree rented a house in the Ojai Valley, where she co-founded The Besant Hill School along with Aldous Huxley, Krishnamurti and others.

"Another link between Iris and Aldous Huxley was that she too had taken mescalin," wrote Richard Morphet. Her biographer Daphne Fielding describes encountering Tree in France where she tried a hallucinogenic mushroom said to produce "beatific visions in glorious Technicolor." Fielding claims Tree didn't really know how to ingest them, but the chapter ends with the suggestion that she'd gone to the Pyrenees because, "Maybe it's good mushroom country."

At the end of her life Tree was forbidden to indulge in cigarettes, coffee and wine for medical reasons. "I feel a traitor," she said "abandoning Baccus the Mind-Shaker and Ganymede the Cup-Bearer." She died in England in 1968, her last words being, "It's here, it's here... Shining...Love...Love...Love."

Photo by Lucien Walery

Josephine Baker
Performer and Humanitarian

The world-famous dancer and singer Josephine Baker indulged in marijuana, according to *Josephine: The Hungry Heart* by Jean-Claude Baker and Chris Chase.

Phillip Leshing, who was then a 23-year-old bass player in Buddy Rich's orchestra, recalls in the book, "I remember once Josephine invited several of us to come to her dressing room and try some very good reefer. I went down with Harry 'Sweets' Edison, the trumpet player, and Buddy Rich, and we smoked pot with Josephine Baker…but the marijuana didn't affect her performance. Never."

According to Leshing, Baker "had this gorgeous gold loving cup made for Buddy and the band, a trophy, like an Academy Award, with our names engraved on it. And it was filled with marijuana. She gave it to us after the last performance at the Strand [the New York club at which they were appearing in March 1951]."

Baker's biographers speculate that she may have first smoked marijuana with her lover Georges Simenon, who used to mix hashish with tobacco in his pipe, or with the Prince of Wales in Paris, in the days when he would come to Le Rat Mort and had to be taken out "feet first every night—dead drunk and stoned," according to another lover, Claude Hopkins.

Born to poor vaudeville entertainers in St. Louis, Missouri, Josephine began working as a live-in maid at the age of eight, and at 13 she quit school and lived on the streets. Her street-corner dancing ultimately landed her in Harlem, and was her ticket to Paris. Ernest Hemingway called her "the most sensational woman anyone ever saw."

Baker adopted more children than Angelina Jolie and was decorated by France for her work for the Resistance. In 1963, she spoke at the March on Washington at the side of Martin Luther King, Jr. wearing her Free French uniform emblazoned with her medal of the Légion d'honneur.

Isak Dinesen

"I suddenly understood everything."

Portrayed by Meryl Streep in *Out of Africa* (1985), based on her 1937 book of the same title, Karen Blixen, known under the pen-name Isak Dinesen and in Africa as Tania, was born in Denmark to a well-off Unitarian family. While running a coffee plantation in Africa, she flew in planes and hunted lions with Denys Finch Hatton.

Dinesen's *Seven Gothic Tales*, published in 1934, was an immediate critical and commercial success in the U.S. She was twice nominated for the Nobel Prize for Literature, and at the end of her life Timothy Leary, Aldous Huxley, Arthur Miller and Marilyn Monroe courted her.

According to *Isak Dinesen, The Life of a Storyteller* by Judith Thurman, Dinesen and Finch Hatton were great fans of Baudelaire, and "Friends remember that Denys and Tania liked to experiment with the sensations hashish, opium, or *miraa* could give them. Denys arranged the cushions on the floor before the fire and reclined there, playing his guitar. Tania sat 'cross-legged like Scheherazade herself' and told him stories." (Miraa is kava, an indigenous African herb that has a mild hallucinogenic effect. Dinesen refers to it in her story "The Dreamers" by its other name, *murungu*.)

"I suddenly understood everything," was a phrase Dinesen used "almost liturgically" in her writing. "It stands for the recognition of a great mystery about oneself, long buried and suddenly come upon again by surprise."

Dinesen wrote to her mother from Africa in 1924, "The greater part of humanity needs excitement, some slight intoxication, pleasure, and danger too. I think that if it were in my power to do anything at all for humanity, I myself would like to amuse them. I think it is wonderful that such delightful peacable people as you exist; but there is need for more than this, and I shall allow myself to make use of Shakespeare's words: 'Dost thou think, because thou are virtuous, there shall be no more cakes and ale? Yes, by St. Anne, and ginger shall be hot I' the mouth too.'"

Photo by Carl Van Vechten / Sponsored by LaTanya Linzie

Bessie Smith

"Gimmie a Reefer"

"Bessie Smith smoked 'reefers' throughout her career, as did many others in the music industry," wrote Buzzy Jackson in *A Bad Woman Feeling Good*. "She was more than merely famous, she was a living symbol of personal freedom: she did what she liked; she spoke her mind, no matter how outrageous her opinion; she flouted bourgeois norms and engaged in alcohol, drugs, and recreational sex."

Born to a large, poor family in Chattanooga, Tennessee, Bessie joined a traveling minstrel show at age 14 and was mentored by Ma Rainey. With her powerful voice, commanding presence, and inventive singing, Smith was soon performing on stages all over the country as The Empress of the Blues, even while the Depression and advent of "talkies" slowed her progress.

In 1933, John Hammond saw Smith perform in a small Philadelphia club and asked her to record four sides for the Okeh label, including "Gimmie a Pigfoot" featuring Benny Goodman and Jack Teagarden. In the last verse, instead of asking for a pigfoot, Smith sings, "Gimmie a reefer."

On September 26, 1937, weeks after the Marijuana Tax Act made marijuana effectively illegal in the U.S., Smith was in a traffic accident and died from her injuries. Some say she was turned away from a "whites only" hospital for treatment. Her funeral was attended by about seven thousand people.

In 1989, Smith was given a Grammy Lifetime Achievement Award and was inducted into the Rock and Roll Hall of Fame. The U.S. Government issued a Bessie Smith postage stamp in 1994.

Queen Latifah, who plays Smith in HBO's *Bessie*, says of her, "If there was a Bessie Smith alive today, she'd blow everyone else out of the water. I could never match her true ability."

Photo: William P. Gottleib

Billie Holiday
"The Loving Type"

"By the 1930s, even before marijuana was criminalized, Billie Holiday's name had become a kind of password among marijuana smokers who had formed an ad hoc network of users across the country," wrote Buzzy Jackson in *A Bad Woman Feeling Good*. The popular singer began to smoke marijuana in the early 1930s when you could buy a couple of joints for twenty-five cents.

At a 1937 recording session, John Hammond managed to convince a record company executive that the marijuana smoke he smelled wasn't a problem. The result was "considered among the greatest recording sessions in jazz history." Holiday's voice interplayed with marijuana-lover Lester Young's saxophone on songs like "I Must Have That Man," leading to a lifelong collaboration.

Holiday was hunted down by no less than Harry J. Anslinger, the first and longtime "drug czar" who engineered laws and international treaties banning marijuana. According to newly published research by Johann Hari, Holiday got her first threat from Anslinger's FBN (Federal Bureau of Narcotics) after she recorded "Strange Fruit," a lament against lynching, in 1939. Anslinger assigned FBN agent Jimmy Fletcher to track Holiday's movements; he tried nailing her but ended up becoming an admirer. "She was the loving type," he wrote.

Billie's manager Louis McKay, who beat her so badly she would have to tape her ribs to go onstage, collaborated with Anslinger to set her up for a heroin bust. Asking to be sent to a treatment facility, she was instead forced to go cold turkey in jail while serving a year's sentence. Later, Anslinger sent another agent to stalk Holiday in San Francisco, possibly planting drugs in her hotel room as he had with others. A jury found her not guilty, but the ordeal took its toll on her reputation and her health.

In 1959, narcotics agents claimed they found a small amount of heroin in Holiday's hospital room. They handcuffed her to her bed and she died there at the age of 44.

Photo: William P. Gottleib

Mary Lou Williams

"Roll 'em"

Born Mary Elfrieda Scruggs in Atlanta, Mary Lou Williams grew up in Pittsburgh, where she taught herself to play the piano at the age of four and began playing publicly two years later. In 1924 she began touring on the Orpheum Circuit and the following year she played with Duke Ellington and the Washingtonians.

In 1930 Williams traveled to Chicago and cut her first solo record, "Drag 'Em" and "Night Life," which was a national success. Soon she was playing solo gigs and working as a freelance writer/arranger for such noteworthy musicians as Earl Hines and Tommy Dorsey. In 1937 she wrote "Roll 'Em" (1937) for Benny Goodman's band, which was recorded for Goodman's "When Buddha Smiles" LP, featuring Fletcher Henderson and Gene Krupa on drums. She wrote more than 350 compositions.

Morning Glory, a biography of Williams by Linda Dahl (University of California Press, 1999), describes a breach between Mary Lou and her first husband John Williams over "the taste she had acquired for marijuana." Dahl wrote, "Kansas City was a major railroad hub of the nation, distributing drugs along with corn and wheat, so it was easily available in the nightclubs there." Unable to handle liquor, pot "agreed with her." John said Mary Lou had been turned on to reefer by a fellow bandmate in the Clouds of Joy, a group that recorded Earl Thompson's song about reefer, "All the Jive Is Gone," in 1936.

Williams "found marijuana calming, useful for reflecting and relaxing at times" (Dahl). By 1941 Mary had developed a lifestyle that disdained alcohol and developed "a taste for gambling, marijuana, and men" but lacked financial security. Barney Josephson fired her for smoking pot one night at Cafe Uptown, even though as Doc Cheatham put it, "everyone in that group smoked pot. They had a little room off the bandstand and some, including Mary Lou and Billie [Holiday], would smoke pot in there. They would put me outside the door in a chair smoking a pipe that would cover the fumes of the pot."

Tallulah Bankhead
"The Champion of Excess"

Tallulah Bankhead was one of the first-ever show business personalities. The daughter of an Alabama Senator, Bankhead won a beauty contest at the age of 16, and headed to New York City to start an acting career. At eighteen she left for Paris to volunteer for the Red Cross.

Around 1918, Bankhead moved into an apartment with actress Bijou Martin, whose wild parties introduced her to cocaine and marijuana. She did abstain from drinking, only because she had promised her father that she would. (Later she drank, to the detriment of her health.)

Bankhead made a name for herself on the London stage and won the New York Drama Critics' Circle Award for *The Little Foxes* on Broadway. She starred in Alfred Hitchcock's film *Lifeboat* and was a well-known radio personality. Said to be the inspiration for Cruella de Vil in Disney's *One Hundred and One Dalmatians*, she was also a real-life inspiration for Bette Davis's role in *All About Eve* (and Davis may have been a model for the young interloper).

A member of the Algonquin Round Table, Tallulah was known for her witticisms, like, "Only good girls keep diaries. Bad girls don't have the time." She also said: "I'm the foe of moderation, the champion of excess. If I may lift a line from a die-hard whose identity is lost in the shuffle, 'I'd rather be strongly wrong than weakly right.'"

In 1948, Bankhead and other cast members were accused of using marijuana during the New York City production of Noel Coward's play *Private Lives*. Bankhead fired her personal secretary, Evyleen Cronin, for stealing money from her in 1951. During a public trial over the incident, Cronin's lawyers alleged that her job included "paying for marijuana, cigarettes, cocaine, booze and sex." Cronin testified that Bankhead taught her to roll marijuana cigarettes.

Bankhead's last words were requests for codeine and bourbon.

Photo: William P. Gottleib

Sarah Vaughan
"The Divine One"

In 1943 Sarah Vaughan (aka "Sassy" or "The Divine One") joined the Earl Hines band, featuring Dizzy Gillespie and Charlie Parker ("Bird"). Gillespie once said, "Sarah can sing notes that other people can't even hear." *Village Voice* jazz critic Gary Giddins said she had "the voice that happens once in a lifetime, perhaps once in several lifetimes."

Sarah wisely never had anything to do with heroin, though "undoubtedly she smoked marijuana with Bird and some of the other men on the road," according to *Sassy: The Life of Sarah Vaughan* by Leslie Gourse. "Sometimes the party was a marathon, with Sassy hanging out for three days at a time, never going to sleep, taking part in every kind of refreshment available—cigarettes, drinks, food, marijuana, maybe cocaine if there was any."

British jazz singer Annie Ross, who worked with Vaughan in the 1950s, was interviewed for Gourse's biography, which says, "As a very young woman, Annie, like Sassy, had enormous energy for a life in the fast lane; together they stayed up all night, drinking and smoking. Sassy liked marijuana and cocaine."

Buster Williams was 20 years old when Vaughan hired him in 1963, generously buying him a bass to play in her band. Gourse writes that Williams smoked marijuana for the first time with Sarah. "She had the uncanny ability to make her voice shimmer," he said.

Vaughan was still enjoying marijuana in April 1989, when Katie Neubauer, an organizer for the Tri C Jazz Fest in Cleveland "was wandering around backstage at the theater when she smelled heady marijuana smoke. She followed the scent to Sassy's dressing room, where the star was also enjoying a glass of brandy. Sassy then walked onstage and gave a magnificent performance."

Sarah's contemporary Ella Fitzgerald recorded "When I Get Low, I Get High" in the 1930s.

Photo: Wikimedia Commons/Michael Williams

Anita O'Day
"Tea for Two"

Known as the Jezebel of Jazz, Anita O'Day was the only white singer in a class with Ella Fitzgerald, Billie Holiday and Sarah Vaughn.

Described not as a mere singer, but rather as musician who used her voice as an instrument, O'Day's rapid-fire delivery could keep up with the likes of Oscar Peterson, Stan Kenton and Gene Krupa. "You can swing, you'd better come with us," Krupa told her when he hired her. Her improvisation skills were such that she once incorporated the rhythm of a ceiling fan into the song.

Rather abandoned as child, O'Day entered Depression-era marathon Walkathons, walking for as many as 2,000 hours to earn food and shelter, and maybe a prize. She started performing in dance contests around the age of 13, smoking reefer with her adult dance partner before they performed (and often won). In those days, you could buy a joint at the corner store, but soon it became illegal. O'Day writes in her autobiography *High Times, Hard Times*, "One day weed had been harmless, booze outlawed; the next, alcohol was in and weed led to 'living death.' They didn't fool me. I kept on using it, but I was just a little more cautious."

Krupa was targeted and arrested for marijuana possession in 1943. "That really bugged me," O'Day writes. "I'd been smoking grass since I was a kid without any terrible effects." She adds in a footnote, "I've always felt that exaggerating the destructive effect of marijuana was a big mistake. The fact that people had used it for years without developing severe problems made it easier for them to discount the physical and economic problems created by use of hard drugs." She soon became a case in point.

O'Day was arrested for pot herself in 1947. She did four months' time, and afterwards was led to heroin, saying, "If they were going to call me a junkie, I figured I might as well be one." After a 16-year addiction, she kicked the habit and came back to tour Japan and Europe, establish two record companies, and write her autobiography.

Simone de Beauvoir

"This substance seems to be less harmful than alcohol."

Simone de Beauvoir, the acclaimed French author whose book *The Second Sex* remains an influential feminist treatise, tried marijuana in New York City in 1947 and wrote about it in her book, *America: Day by Day*.

"As in all big cities, people use a lot of drugs in New York," de Beauvoir wrote. "Cocaine, opium, and heroin have a specialized clientele, but there's a mild stimulant that's commonly used, even though it's illegal—marijuana. Almost everywhere, especially in Harlem (their economic status leads many blacks into illegal drug trafficking), marijuana cigarettes are sold under the counter. Jazz musicians who need to maintain a high level of intensity for nights at a time use it readily. It hasn't been found to cause any physiological problems...this substance seems to be less harmful than alcohol."

De Beauvoir says she was "less interested in tasting marijuana itself than in being at one of the gatherings where it's smoked." As she describes it, she valiantly tried smoking four cigarettes and failed to feel any effect." But during the next few days, "I live in a half-dream; perhaps the marijuana smoke insidiously slipped into my blood," she wrote. She authored *The Second Sex* the following year, with fresh revelations about the female condition.

"In the Middle Ages, and in the Renaissance, the female physician had much power," de Beauvoir said in a 1975 television interview. "They knew about remedies and herbs, the 'old wives' remedies which were sometimes of great value. Then medicine was taken away from them by men. All of the witch hunts were basically a way for men to keep women away from medicine and the power it conferred. In the 18th and 19th centuries statutes were drafted by men that prevented women—who were imprisoned, fined, etc. —from practicing medicine unless they had attended certain schools, which did not admit them anyway. Women were relegated to the role of nurses, of Florence Nightingale, as aides and assistants."

Lila Leeds
"She Shoulda Said No"

Starlet Lila Leeds was 20 years old when she was arrested with Robert Mitchum for marijuana in 1948. While Mitchum's star power—and the money the studios had invested in him—carried him through the ordeal that followed, Leeds never recovered from the incident.

Under contract to MGM, one of Leeds's bit parts was in the Lana Turner vehicle *Green Dolphin Street*, where she plays a Eurasian woman who drugs the leading man and rolls him. There was no question Lila had a face, and a figure, to rival Lana.

Having been turned on to reefer by Stan Kenton's orchestra, "Lila had always been jazz-happy and she knew many of the local musicians," wrote Lee Server in *Robert Mitchum: Baby I Don't Care*. "She smoked reefers with them in their dressing rooms and in the parking lots, even at the tables if the owners were cool."

"I smoked socially," Lila said. "The way some people take a drink. Pot doesn't affect me much—just makes me sleepy and relaxed."

At the time of her arrest with Mitchum, Leeds was engaged to Turner's ex-husband Steven Crane. Their daughter Cheryl Crane's book *Detour: A Hollywood Story* says that Leeds was introduced to heroin by fellow inmates at the LA County Jail, and it led to addiction.

In a police deposition, Leeds accused her roommate Vicki Evans of being a police informer, and said that Mitchum was framed for the offense. Neither Evans nor bartender Robin Ford, who brought Mitchum to the scene of the arrest, were tried for the incident.

Other than the awful Reefer Madness-style anti-drug film *She Shoulda Said No*, Leeds never had another film role. She became so destitute that she hocked the three-carat diamond ring Crane had given her for $750. In the 1970s, she worked as a faith healer for addicts.

Candy Barr

"I was holding it for a friend (in my bra)."

The erotic dancer known as Candy Barr was born Juanita Dale Slusher in Edna, Texas. After her mother died when she was nine, she was ignored by a new stepmother and sexually abused by a neighbor and a babysitter. She ran away and took various jobs, eventually developing her striptease act and trademark costume: a 10-gallon hat, pasties, "scanty panties," a pair of six-shooters and cowboy boots.

Barr tried stage acting, but her legitimate career was derailed in 1957, when she was arrested for having a little less than four-fifths of an ounce of marijuana concealed in her bra. She maintained that she was framed by police and was only holding it for a friend, but was convicted and sentenced to 15 years in prison.

"I always wanted a brick house of my own, and it looks like I am going to have one," Barr told an assembled crowd and news media when she walked into Goree Farm for Women in Huntsville, Texas in 1959. During her imprisonment, she took high school courses, worked as a seamstress, sang in the prison choir, and played in its band.

Before her incarceration Barr trained actress Joan Collins for her role as an exotic dancer in the 1960 movie *Seven Thieves*, earning her a credit as technical adviser. "She taught me more about sensuality than I had learned in all my years under contract," Collins wrote in her autobiography, *Past Imperfect*.

Then-Texas Gov. John B. Connally paroled Barr in 1963 and pardoned her four years later. Barr was arrested a second time for possession of marijuana in a 1969 raid on her home, but charges were dropped for lack of evidence.

In 1984, *Texas Monthly* listed Barr among such luminaries as Lady Bird Johnson as one of history's "perfect Texans." A Candy Barr biopic was contemplated in 1980 starring fellow Texan Farrah Fawcett, but the project was scrapped.

Photo: Wikipedia Commons

Margaret Mead

"Marihuana is not harmful unless it is taken in enormous and excessive amounts."

Margaret Mead was the most famous anthropologist in the world, and her books like *Coming of Age in Samoa* helped bring about the sexual revolution of the 1960s.

Mead taught at a number of institutions, authored some twenty books and co-authored an equal number. She served as president of the American Anthropological Association and the American Association for the Advancement of Science, and she received 28 honorary doctorates.

Mead testified before Congress in favor of the legalization of marijuana on October 27, 1969, and she told *Newsweek* in 1970 that she had tried it once herself. In her testimony, Mead said, "It is my considered opinion at present that marihuana is not harmful unless it is taken in enormous and excessive amounts. I believe that we are damaging this country, damaging our law, our whole law enforcement situation, damaging the trust between the older people and younger people by its prohibition, and this is far more serious than any damage that might be done to a few overusers, because you can get damage from any kind of overuse."

"We occasionally find a society that will reject anything that leads to any kind of ecstatic state or of people ever getting outside of themselves," Mead continued. "But in general man has sought for ways of changing his moods, of making it possible for him to work longer than he could, to stay up longer than he could, to get through a meeting or a tremendous bout of work better than he could have otherwise....In the West Indies, people smoke marihuana to get through a hard day's work and after they have done the hard day's work they smoke another bit of marihuana to relax and enjoy the evening."

Among her many accolades, Mead was awarded the Presidential Medal of Freedom following her death in 1978.

Photo: Grunt Records, 1977

Grace Slick

"Remember what the dormouse said. Feed your head."

Raised in the San Francisco Bay Area, Grace Wing discovered marijuana in 1958 at the University of Miami, where she was enrolled. In 1961 she married Jerry Slick, a film student at San Francisco State College. The two rented a house in Potrero Hill where "we'd grow dope in the backyard, for our own entertainment," said Grace in *Got a Revolution! The Turbulent Flight of Jefferson Airplane* by Jeff Tamarkin.

Grace found the Beatles early songs childish and preferred Bartok, Prokofiev, the musical *South Pacific,* and jazz, in particular Miles Davis's *Sketches of Spain*. With her husband and his brother, she formed a band in the Summer of 1965 called *The Great Society,* after LBJ's disdained social program. She soon brought her talents to the *Jefferson Airplane,* one of the seminal bands of the San Francisco music scene.

Drawing on her love of Spanish songs, Grace used a bolero rhythm for a song that became an anthem for a generation:
One pill makes you larger and one pill makes you small
And the ones that Mother gives you don't do anything at all
Go ask Alice, when she's ten feet tall

Slick said, "The parents read us these books, like *Alice in Wonderland,* where she gets high, tall, and she takes mushrooms, a hookah, pills, alcohol. And then there's the *Wizard of Oz,* where they fall into a field of poppies and when they wake up they see Oz. And then there's *Peter Pan,* where if you sprinkle white dust on you, you could fly. And then you wonder why we do it? Well, what did you read to me?"

Slick has now put down the microphone and picked up a paintbrush, and her visual art is as provocative and powerful as her music. She visually recorded the Monterey Pop festival in one painting, and in another a character named "Rescue Rabbit" carries cannabis to the Capitol building in DC. She has donated proceeds from her paintings to the Marijuana Policy Project.

Janis Joplin

"I spend my money all on Mary Jane."

Janis Joplin was an outcast "beatnik" who "wore the black leotards" and smoked weed while in high school in Port Arthur, Texas. No one gave more of herself in her art, and still never felt appreciated. "Onstage, I make love to 25,000 people—then I go home alone," she once said.

Even the song Joplin wrote and recorded about weed laments its popularity. In a blues song often misattributed to her heroine Bessie Smith (p. 54), Janis sang:

Now when I go to work, I work all day.
Always turns out the same.
When I bring home my hard earned pay,
I spend my money all on Mary Jane.
Mary Jane, Mary Jane, lord, my Mary Jane.

Oh, Elizabeth Taylor, Marilyn Monroe
They all turn out the same.
'cause they can't do nothing to make a man feel good
Like my old Mary Jane

On a Dick Cavett episode filmed just two months before her brightly burning candle burned out, Joplin gives an astonishing performance of "Half Moon," showing she's in full control of her tight-as-a-drum band, the aptly named *Full Tilt Boogie*. Afterwards, she stands up for pot to fellow guest Gloria Swanson, talking about repression in the 1920s when Swanson was making movies. "Back then you couldn't drink because they didn't like it. Now you can't smoke grass," Janis said. "Back then you couldn't be a flapper because they didn't like it, and now you can't play rock and roll....It seems to me that people who went through all that prohibition and flapper times should realize that young people are always crazy, and to leave us alone."

In 2014, the USPS issued a postage stamp in Janis's honor.

Mama Cass Elliot

"A mind of her own."

"Mama" Cass Elliot was by all accounts an exceptionally intelligent, talented, and giving individual. Witty and captivating, with perfect pitch and impeccable timing, Cass was eventually paid court to by David Crosby, Graham Nash, the Beatles, Dave Mason, Graham Parsons, Donovan, Eric Clapton, and many others. She introduced Crosby to Nash and Nash to LSD. Contemporary artists from Boy George and k.d. lang to Anthony Kiedis of the Red Hot Chili Peppers cite Cass as an influence.

The teenager named Ellen Cohen found her way to Baltimore's downtown, with its beatnik society, after the Dexedrene she was prescribed as a diet drug made her too jumpy to stay in school. She began to explore poetry readings, bookshops, and cafes of the neighborhood, smoking hash and grass at her friends' apartments afterwards.

She soon changed her name and headed to New York, forming the folk trio The Big 3, once "magically" creating a hash pipe, complete with bowl and stem, out of the foil lining from a pack of cigarettes at a Big 3 recording session.

It was Cass who came up with the name "The Mamas and the Papas," and her powerful vocals drove the group. According to Michelle Phillips, Cass was by far the most popular member, getting oodles more fan mail than the other three. Many who knew her called her the Gertrude Stein of her generation for her frequent parties.

Cass became active in the 1972 McGovern for President campaign and said, "I think that I would like to be a senator or something in twenty years." It later emerged that the FBI had been monitoring Cass. FBI sources uncovered that she was of "the hippie generation," had allegedly smoked marijuana, was "very independent" and had "a mind of her own."

Barbra Streisand

"It's still illegal?"

Barbra, The Way She Is by Christopher Anderson recounts how while playing Vegas in 1970, La Streisand voiced jealousy of Dean Martin and the Rat Packers who drank onstage. Announcing her preferred method of relaxation was grass, she lit up onstage, leading groups like Little Anthony and the Imperials to send her the "best pot." The book also says her role in *The Way We Were* was dependent on her appearing at a McGovern rally organized by Warren Beatty on April 15, 1972.

According to David Crosby's book, *Stand and Be Counted*, after a second standing ovation at the McGovern event, Streisand stopped to talk to the crowd. Speaking of her stage fright, she said, "I was even more scared until I spoke to friends of mine, also performers you know, and they were telling me...that in order to conquer their fear...some of them drink. But I really hate the taste of liquor so I can't do that. Some of them take pills, but I can't even take aspirin."

At that moment she took an exaggerated drag of what appeared to be a joint. After huge laugher and applause, she made a confused face and asked, "It's still illegal?" Taking another toke she said through clenched teeth (as though holding the smoke in), "We should face our problems head on." She then sang, "On a Clear Day You Can See Forever" and received a total of six standing ovations.

Streisand's first husband Elliot Gould said in 1974, "I have no problem with drugs." "Not even marijuana?" he was asked. "No one has a problem with marijuana," he replied. Her current husband James Brolin played a pivotal role as an outgoing drug "czar" in the anti-drug-war movie *Traffic* (2000).

Streisand recently appeared as Seth Rogen's mother in the 2012 film *The Guilt Trip*, in which her character drinks when she needs to blow off steam, instead of using something more interesting. Asked whether or not they toked together on the set, Rogen said, "No, but we talked about it a lot," adding, "She smoked weed with Peter Sellers though."

Sue Mengers

"The big thing was grass. It was like a ceremony."

The first "superagent," Sue Mengers began as a secretary in 1955 at MCA and ended up representing, among many others, megastars like Barbra Streisand, Candice Bergen, Cher, Faye Dunaway, and Gore Vidal. "She was one of a kind, acerbically funny, witty, brash, tough but cuddly, a powerful woman in a man's world," said Streisand.

Mengers' pot smoking was well known; it was joked that to get a job working for her, one had to know how to roll joints. Mailroom workers noticed marijuana inside packages sent from the William Morris agency where she worked to her home. "She always had the joints rolled, and kept them in a little box in the coffee table," said fellow pot-lover Bill Maher.

Forced out by the good old boys of William Morris, Mengers bounced back by holding dinner parties in Beverly Hills that were legendary. She "became one of Beverly Hills' top hostesses, with A-List stars crowding her dinner parties and Mengers (joint in hand) at the center of it all," wrote Josh Ferri at Broadway.com.

"She was the modern-day Gertrude Stein," said CBS President Leslie Moonves. "People would gather and exchange ideas and talk about things that were not talked about anywhere else in town."

"The big thing was grass," said Mengers. "It was like a ceremony. People sat on the floor, you'd smoke a joint."

Bette Midler won rave reviews playing Mengers in the one-woman Broadway show, *I'll Eat You Last* in 2013. "Midler's Mengers passes the 90-minute show lounging on a couch, puffing on a joint, pumping out profane one-liners," wrote *The Week*. Charles Isherwood of the *New York Times* wrote, "Ms. Midler...gives the most lusciously entertaining performance of the Broadway season...She cradles a spellbound audience in the palm of her hand from first joke to last toke."

84 Tokin' Women: A 4000-Year Herstory

Photofest / Sponsored by: M&M Aldrich

Elizabeth Taylor

"They were high on pot a lot."

Elizabeth Taylor is remembered for her addictions to alcohol and painkillers, often prescribed to keep her films shooting on schedule. According to one biographer, she also smoked pot.

Ellis Amburn's *The Most Beautiful Woman in the World* says Taylor's experimentation with marijuana began in mid-1973, when she partied with Peter Lawford and his son Christopher, hitting hot spots like The Candy Store in Beverly Hills. Peter's friend Arthur Natoli recalled, "[Christopher] and Elizabeth used to turn on together. They were high on pot a lot."

Taylor was 19 when she was cast in *A Place in the Sun* opposite Montgomery Clift, and she had a lifelong devotion to Clift, who smoked marijuana (as did James Dean). According to Amburn, "Elizabeth sometimes ditched [second husband Michael] Wilding to slip off to Oscar Levant's Beverly Hills house with Monty, where the pianist serenaded them with Gershwin tunes as they whiled away afternoons and early evenings." Sounds like a pothead's dream date to me.

Taylor's fourth husband Eddie Fisher is revealed as a pot smoker by his daughter Carrie in her 2008 book *Wishful Drinking*. "You would just love him," Fisher writes of her "Puff Daddy."

Liz played a free-spirited artist living in Carmel, CA in 1965's *The Sandpiper* (pictured), which features a discussion of Dionysian pleasures. In 1989 she appeared as the aging actress Alexandra Del Lago—who a young hustler tries to smear because of her hashish habit—in a TV version of Tennessee Williams's play *Sweet Bird of Youth*.

Taylor won several humanitarian awards for her work raising over $10 million and much awareness for AIDS at a time when no one wanted to acknowledge the disease. Lately, Christopher Lawford has joined with Senator Patrick Kennedy to form the anti-marijuana group SAM.

Linda McCartney

"I think marijuana is pretty lightweight."

The classy lady who married the world's most eligible bachelor (Paul McCartney) was a well-known rock photographer when they met. Linda Eastman photographed the Rolling Stones during their visit to New York and also captured images of Janis Joplin, Bob Dylan, the Doors, the Grateful Dead, and the Mamas and the Papas. Her work appeared in *Rolling Stone*, *Life*, and other leading magazines.

Linda later reminisced about smoking pot in Central Park on her way to her studio. "Lovely times," she said. Perhaps taking the rap for Paul, Linda was arrested in Los Angeles in 1975 for marijuana possession, but the charges were dropped. Reportedly she and Paul never spent a night away from each other after their marriage, except for his ten-day stint in a Tokyo jail for possession of marijuana in 1980.

In 1984, the McCartneys were arrested in Barbados for possession of marijuana and were fined $100 each. They flew to Heathrow Airport, London, where Linda was arrested again on charges of possession. Rather than repudiate her marijuana use as so many do, Linda commented, "I think hard drugs are disgusting. But I must say, I think marijuana is pretty lightweight."

A vegetarian, McCartney wrote several cookbooks and developed a successful line of frozen meat-free meals. She was an active member of PETA, or People for the Ethical Treatment of Animals, was also involved in environmental causes, and raised four children. The world mourned when she died of breast cancer in 1998.

After Linda's death, Paul married the now-discredited Heather Mills, who he divorced just after she said she wouldn't tolerate his marijuana smoking. Afterwards he stepped away briefly from his longstanding vocal support for marijuana legalization during a custody battle over his daughter with Mills, perhaps making him one of the most high-profile parents to have this all-too-common problem.

Photo: G. Paul Bishop / Sponsored by LaTanya Linzie

Maya Angelou

"I felt I was in a charcoal sketch, or a sepia watercolor."

Revered author Maya Angelou, the first poet since Robert Frost to read a poem at a Presidential inauguration, wrote about her experiences with marijuana in *Gather Together in My Name*, the second installment of her autobiography after the acclaimed *I Know Why the Caged Bird Sings*.

Angelou, who started life as Rita Johnson from Stamps, Arkansas, was raped at the age of 7, and had an illegitimate child in her teens. Working as a waitress to support her son in San Diego, 18-year-old Rita met two lesbian prostitutes who frequented the bar where she worked. One night, the women invited her to their house for dinner and invited her to smoke *grifa* with them. Afterwards, Angelou recounts:

"The food was the best I'd ever tasted. Every morsel was an experience of sheer delight. I lost myself in a haze of sensual pleasure, enjoying not only the tastes but the feel of the food in my mouth, the smells, and the sound of my jaws chewing...I decided to dance for my hostesses. The music dipped and swayed, pulling and pushing. I let my body rest on the sound and turned and bowed in the tiny room. The shapes and forms melted until I felt I was in a charcoal sketch, or a sepia watercolor."

Later, while working as a waitress, she wrote, "Smoking grass eased the strain for me...From a natural stiffness I melted into a grinning tolerance. Walking on the streets became high adventure, eating my mother's huge dinners an opulent entertainment, and playing with my son was side-cracking hilarity. For the first time, life amused me...

"I disciplined myself. One joint on Sunday and one on the morning of my day off. The weed always had an intense and immediate effect. Before the cigarette was smoked down to roach length, I had to smother my giggles. Just to see the falling folds of the curtains or the sway of a chair was enough to bring me to audible laughter."

Karen Silkwood

American Heroine

Union organizer and activist Karen Silkwood worked as a technician at the Cimarron plutonium plant operated by Kerr-McGee near Crescent, Oklahoma. The first woman to serve as a member of the bargaining committee of the Oil, Chemical & Atomic Workers Union, she was charged with investigating health and safety issues at the plant.

In the summer of 1974, Silkwood testified to the Atomic Energy Commission that she had found serious violations of health and safety regulations—including evidence of spills, leaks, faulty fuel rods and enough missing plutonium to make multiple nuclear weapons. She also alleged the company had falsified inspection records.

A few months later, Silkwood was found dead after her car went off the road into a ditch. A manila envelope carrying documents about corruption at the Kerr-McGee plant was never found afterwards, but investigators did find marijuana cigarettes in the pocket of her coat.

In the 1983 movie *Silkwood*, Karen (played by Meryl Streep) shares a joint with her boyfriend (Kurt Russell) and roommate (Cher) in the same car she is driving when she dies.

Karen's death at the age of 28 in 1974 led to a national discussion about nuclear plant safety, the ultimate closure of the Oklahoma plant where she worked, and a million-dollar settlement in a lawsuit brought by her family.

Silkwood helped immortalize the courageous Karen Silkwood. Did her pot smoking make her more attuned to the greater issues around her, as so often happens with the cannabis-initiated? If so, it's one more reason why marijuana is considered dangerous to the status quo, and why it's so important for all of us to get past the cruel prejudice against it and on to the greater issues at hand.

Jennifer Aniston

"I enjoy it once in a while. There's nothing wrong with that."

Raised in New York, Los Angeles, and Greece, Jennifer Aniston had her first taste of acting at age 11 when she joined the Rudolf Steiner School's drama club, and she began her professional training as a drama student at New York's High School of the Performing Arts. In 1987, after graduation, she started appearing in off-Broadway productions and television.

In 1994, she was asked to audition for the role of Monica for a TV pilot called *Friends Like These*. Aniston refused and won instead the role of Rachel Green, the suburban princess turned coffee peddler. She was the only *Friends* cast member to win an Emmy and go on to a successful film career.

Aniston told *Rolling Stone* (September 27, 2001): "I wouldn't call myself a pothead. I mean, I enjoy it once in a while. There's nothing wrong with that. Everything in moderation." Commenting on anonymous reports in the tabloids about Aniston and then-husband Brad Pitt's "drug use," Aniston said, "You see something like that—me and my husband, hooked on drugs. Then you read the story, and it says you smoke pot. It's not even cocaine or shooting heroin. Pot!"

In the 2014 film *Life of Crime*, Aniston's character has a little fun laughing at the classic *Sanford and Son* scene involving marijuana. In the film, as so often in life, smoking a little weed leads to a woman looking at the world in a different, better way.

In a role for which she was nominated for numerous awards, Aniston plays a woman who suffers from chronic pain in *Cake*. Too bad the woman she played didn't try cannabis, since research shows it's helpful for pain patients and works synergistically with opiates.

In 2015, Jen had some fun in a "lip flip" with *Tonight Show* host Jimmy Fallon, declaring her support for the Seattle Seahawks in the Superbowl because, "We got the weed, man!" She's married Justin Theroux, who played a hippie she has a fling with in *Wanderlust* (2012).

Photo: Galbraith/AP Sponsored by Paradigm Cannabis Group

Whoopi Goldberg

"And honey, when they called my name…"

Born Caryn Johnson, Whoopi Goldberg's unique talent and voice have made her one of the few entertainers to hit a Grand Slam: she's won a Grammy, an Oscar, a Tony, and two Emmys.

Her Grammy came for the 1985 recording of her one-woman show *Direct from Broadway* that cemented her place in the comedy stratosphere, with an amazing range and depth of characters, including a Jamaican Rastaman and the angry young junkie Fontaine.

While Goldberg was highly praised for her lead role in the adaptation of Alice Walker's *The Color Purple* (1985), it was her portrayal of a wacky medium in *Ghost* (1990) that earned her an Oscar. She was later caught on tape saying she smoked "the last of her homegrown" before giving perhaps the most sincere Oscar acceptance speech ever, with glistening eyes. She was only the second black woman to win an Oscar. (Hattie McDaniel was the first for *Gone With the Wind*.)

Goldberg, who dropped out of high school and became a heroin addict in her teens, has spoken openly about her past. She won an Emmy for Outstanding Talk Show Host for *The View* in 2009, the same year she defended Michael Phelps's famous post-Olympic bong hit on the show, outing herself on the air by saying, "God help me, I'm going to make an admission and I hope you all are sitting down. I have smoked weed."

Five years later, she became a columnist for the Denver Post's pot site, *The Cannabist*, debuting with an article titled "My Vape Pen and I, a Love Story" that revealed her use of marijuana for glaucoma. "The vape pen has changed my life," she wrote. "I named her Sippy because I take tiny, little sips—sassy sips, even—from her. And with each sip comes relief—from pressure, pain, stress, discomfort."

In March 2016, Goldberg announced that her company Maya & Whoopi would market cannabis products to treat menstrual cramps.

Photo: Dean Chalkley. Sponsored by GreenFlashGlass.com

Chrissie Hynde

"Legalise Me. I want the legal right to be me."

With a voice and a sense of purpose that won't quit, rock mama Chrissie Hynde is often cited as an influence on younger female musicians, but as Branford Marsalis once introduced her on *The Tonight Show*, she is "Incomparable."

Born in Akron, Ohio, Hynde bought a one-way ticket to London where she became a rock critic before founding her band The Pretenders. Her breakthrough hit "Brass in Pocket" might have been written to get the attention of Ray Davies of The Kinks. If so, it worked: she had his child. Hynde took several years off from touring to raise her daughters, and her album "Learning to Crawl" documents the experience as only Chrissie could. She recorded a beautiful version of Dylan's tune "Forever Young" and the lyrics to her song "I'll Stand By You" gain an extra poignancy when they seem to be aimed at a child.

Hynde has never been afraid to voice her opinions concerning causes she believes strongly about, such as ending animal cruelty. In October 1997 Hynde appeared on the cover of *High Times*, speaking in favor of marijuana legalization. In November of that year, during a California concert held on National Medical Marijuana Day, she and dreamboat drummer Martin Chambers wore green ribbons onstage. Hynde stopped the show to announce that it was because, "We do endorse the use of the herb for medical and other reasons. And I can tell you at 46 that marijuana is the key to longevity." Then she said, "And this is for the Freedom Fighters," and played her song "Revolution."

Hynde's song "Legalise Me" has the lyric:
I don't take Prozac and I'll never own a gun
I'm just a farmer and I grow marijuana

Her 2014 follow up, "Dark Sunglasses" seems to have a similar, more subtle message. In her 2015 autobiography *Reckless* she writes about coming home to Ohio where she brought European-style spliffs (complete with tobacco) and became "a bit of a cultural ambassador."

Susan Blackmore

"Without cannabis, most of my scientific research would never have been done."

Psychologist Susan Blackmore, author of the bestselling book *The Meme Machine,* has over 650,000 views on her TED Talk on "Memes and Temes." At the 2005 Cheltenham Science Festival, discussing whether drugs can teach us anything about ourselves, she said:

"Some people may smoke dope just to relax or have fun, but for me the reason goes deeper. In fact, I can honestly say that without cannabis, most of my scientific research would never have been done and most of my books on psychology and evolution would not have been written....Some evenings, after a long day at my desk, I'll slip into the bath, light a candle and a spliff, and let the ideas flow—that lecture I have to give to 500 people next week, that article I'm writing for *New Scientist,* those tricky last words of a book I've been working on for months. This is the time when the sentences seem to write themselves. Or I might sit out in my greenhouse on a summer evening among my tomatoes and peach trees, struggling with questions about free will or the nature of the universe, and find that a smoke gives me new ways of thinking about them.

"In just about every human society there has ever been, people have used dangerous drugs – but most have developed rituals that bring an element of control or safety to the experience," Blackmore continued. "In more primitive societies, it is shamans and healers who control the use of dangerous drugs, choose appropriate settings in which to take them and teach people how to appreciate the visions and insights that they can bring. In our own society, criminals control all drug sales. This means that users have no way of knowing exactly what they are buying and no one to teach them how to use these dangerous tools...

"It's an old metaphor, but people often liken the task to climbing a mountain. The drugs can take you up in a helicopter to see what's there, but you can't stay. In the end, you have to climb the mountain yourself—the hard way. Even so, by giving you that first glimpse, the drugs may provide the inspiration to keep climbing."

Photo: Daigo Oliva, Wikipedia Commons

Patti Smith

"Somewhere along the line I decided to try their sacred herb."

I read Nerval's Women of Cairo, *and the stories of Bowles, Mrabet, Albert Cossery, and Isabelle Eberhardt. Since hashish permeated the atmosphere of these stories I had it in my mind to partake of it.*

So writes Patti Smith in her bestselling book *Just Kids*, about her relationship with Robert Mapplethorpe and her early days as a writer and musician in New York. He was on acid the day they hooked up, but was still shocked when he found she was smoking pot, as Smith relates in her book:

"Patti, no!" Robert gasped. "You're smoking pot!" I looked up sheepishly. Busted.

I had seen The Harder They Come, *and was stirred by the music... I found irresistible the Rastafarian connection to Solomon and Sheba, and the Abyssinia of Rimbaud, and somewhere along the line I decided to try their sacred herb...*

With Robert, I was not transported into the Abyssinian plain, but into the valley of uncontrollable laughter. I told him that pot was supposed to be for writing poetry, not fooling around. But all we did was laugh...

"I never thought of pot as a social drug. I liked to use it to work, to think, and eventually for improvising with [musicians] Lenny Kaye and Richard Sohl as the three of us would gather under a frankincense tree dreaming of Haile Selassie."

Smith's is not a tale of overindulgence in drugs. It is instead one of a dedicated artist who witnessed some of the excesses of drug use, and experimented herself deliberately and thoughtfully.

Known as the "punk poet laureate," Smith was named a Commander of the Ordre des Arts et des Lettres by the French Ministry of Culture in 2005, and in 2007 she was inducted into the Rock and Roll Hall of Fame. She won the National Book Award for *Just Kids*.

Sarah Palin

"I can't claim
a Bill Clinton
and say I
never inhaled."

When Sarah Palin smoked pot in Alaska, it was legal to do so (and it is again, as of November 2014). A 1975 Alaska Supreme Court decision had allowed adults to possess small amounts of marijuana for personal use under the state constitutional right to privacy. Our first drug "czar" Bill Bennett resigned calling the drug war won after Alaska voters passed a 1990 ballot initiative re-criminalizing the herb. An appeals court overturned the voters in 2003 but in June 2006, a law signed by then-Governor Frank Murkowski re-criminalized it again.

Then-Alaska Governor Palin outed herself during a 2006 interview in the *Alaska Daily News*. "I can't claim a Bill Clinton and say that I never inhaled," she told the paper. She added that she didn't like it and doesn't smoke it now. (Politicians seem to be the only creatures who don't like smoking pot. How convenient.)

While running for governor, Palin said she didn't support legalizing marijuana, worrying about the message it would send to her children. But the former GOP Vice Presidential candidate became part of the Marijuana Majority when she said: "We need to prioritize our law enforcement efforts, and if somebody's gonna smoke a joint in their house and not do anybody else any harm, then perhaps there are other things that our cops should be looking at to engage in and try to clean up some of the other problems that we have in society that are appropriate for law enforcement to do."

Palin's father, a schoolteacher, protected his children against the most dangerous drug of all: television. He unplugged the family TV set and put it away during the summer, forcing Sarah and her siblings to play outside and read for their amusement.

At least three biographies of Democratic presidential candidate Hillary Clinton say she enjoyed pot during her college days, but she told CNN's Christiane Amanpour she never inhaled. She did call the states "laboratories of democracy" on full legalization.

Melissa Etheridge

"I don't want to look like a criminal to my children anymore."

In an interview that aired October 16, 2005 on *Dateline NBC*, singer/songwriter Melissa Etheridge said she smoked medicinal marijuana to help with the side effects of chemotherapy during her treatment for breast cancer.

"Instead of taking five or six of the prescriptions, I decided to go a natural route and smoke marijuana," Etheridge said. She added that she smoked every day for her pain and symptoms and "the minute I didn't feel it, I stopped." (This immediate relief is why smoking is such an effective way to ingest marijuana, rather than taking it orally.)

Etheridge said every doctor she asked responded, "Oh, yeah. That's the best help for the effects of chemotherapy."

Etheridge appeared at an LA press conference in October 2010 in support of Proposition 19, a measure that sought to legalize marijuana for adult, recreational use in California. "I don't want to look like a criminal to my children anymore," she stated. "I want them to know this is a choice that you make as a responsible adult."

Etheridge was interviewed in *High Times's* 420th issue (January 2011) where she noted that "America has always had a pot culture" and said, "I was on chemotherapy, and it was horrible. But the pain was alleviated by cannabis. It was awesome—truly. I was able to sit there and really see that health is just balance. Cannabis helps balance. If we had reputable tests done on stress and cannabis alleviation of pain, doctors would prescribe it all the time—and they should." She added, "I'm very much a sativa girl, the indicas just put me to sleep."

In 2014, Etheridge announced she was developing a cannabis-infused wine. She performed rockin' covers of Brandy Clark's "Get High" and Bob Marley's "Get Up, Stand Up" at a Grammy Museum-sponsored Concert for Social Justice in April 2015, where she pronounced the cannabis revolution "is being won by middle-aged women."

Photofest / Sponsored by: Giggle Therapeutics

Lily Tomlin

"It's so hard to get good grass these days."

Lily Tomlin's character "The Tasteful Lady" is a great send-up of the kind of "Mothers Against Everything" that would put the clampdown on cannabis. Her masterful album "Modern Scream" asks this mock question:
> Interviewer: "Lily, is it true you have a drug problem?"
> Lily: "Yes, it's so hard to get good grass these days."

As one of the two Tokin' Women (along with Joan Rivers) honoring George Carlin when he posthumously won the Mark Twain Prize, Tomlin opened with, "I flatter myself to think that George and I somehow drank from the same comedy fountain. Or should I say 'inhaled'? Or perhaps I shouldn't."

Lily inhales on screen with Dolly Parton and Jane Fonda in the 1980 movie *9 to 5*, after her screen son rolls her one. "You're the one who keeps saying harm springs from excess," he tells her. "I'm talking about one joint." Playing Lisa Kudrow's mom Putsy on Showtime's *Web Therapy* (shown), Tomlin tokes up and declares, "I've always absolutely loved pot all my life—and the Thai stick." On *The Jimmy Kimmel Show*, she set up a mock cannabis dispensary in her dressing room.

Tomlin fully "outed" herself as a pot smoker in the October 2012 issue of *Culture* magazine. Asked if she's an advocate for marijuana legalization, Tomlin replied, "Yes, yes. Of course." To the question, does she have any favorite cannabis strains, Tomlin replied, "I wish I was that sophisticated."

Fonda and Tomlin reunite onscreen in the Netflix series *Grace and Frankie*. In the first episode, the two take a peyote trip with the prelude, "Brace yourself for some light vomiting, followed by life-altering hallucinations." In Episode 4 when Grace (Fonda) says to Frankie (Tomlin), "All your clothes reek of pot," she replies, "Because I wear hemp and not dead snakes on my feet." Tomlin received an Emmy nomination for her role. She won a Kennedy Center Award in 2014.

Jane Fonda

"You don't mind if I turn on, do you?"

Just before Jane Fonda controversially played Nancy Reagan, she did a turn as a hippie grandmother named Grace in 2011's *Peace, Love, & Misunderstanding* (pictured). Grace, whose home smells of pot, deals a little on the side and introduces her grandkids to the wonders of the weed. It's done intelligently, with Grace resorting to the initiation before losing them to an evening of watching them close down (as so many teens do). Afterwards, she gives them sage advice: stay away from the brown stuff (heroin) and nothing up the nose (cocaine).

It's the first Fonda has toked on film since *9 to 5*, where she plays an innocent who finds her inner strength with the aid of weed and some gal pals, just before they take on their boorish boss. The movie helped launch the SEIU (Service Employees International Union).

In 1969, the year she won a well-deserved Oscar for *They Shoot Horses, Don't They?*, Fonda asked critic Rex Reed before he interviewed her, "You don't mind if I turn on, do you?" Fonda was observed smoking some weed at a recent Oscar party and has admitted she still smokes from time to time.

The child of a famously stoic movie icon father and a beautiful mother who killed herself when Jane was 12, she played out her relationship with her dad on screen in *On Golden Pond*. She's still vilified as "Hanoi Jane," even though she spent the war years advocating for veterans. Her thoughtful film about the Vietnam War, *Coming Home*, was trounced at the Oscars in favor of the controversial *The Deer Hunter*.

Fonda was great as Tokin' Woman Lillian Hellman in *Julia*, and in her recent turn as a network executive on HBO's *The Newsroom*, where her character jokes about dealing "a little pot" to win back her network. The role is doubtlessly informed by her marriage to CNN's Ted Turner. She was also married to SDS leader and former California Assemblyman Tom Hayden.

Photo sponsored by Kyndra Miller

Oprah Winfrey

"I hear it's gotten better."

Oprah Winfrey was asked when she last smoked marijuana on Bravo's "Watch What Happens Live" in August 2013. She replied "Uh...1982." Host Andy Cohen then said, "Let's hang out after the show" to which she replied, "Okay. I hear it's gotten better."

At age 17, Winfrey won the Miss Black Tennessee beauty pageant and soon became the first black female news anchor at Nashville's WLAC-TV. According to Kitty Kelley's unauthorized biography, drug use was so prevalent at the Nashville station when Oprah worked there that management removed a vending machine "after they discovered it had been rigged to dispense marijuana."

In 1983, Winfrey began to host AM Chicago, beginning her metioric rise to fame, fortune and influence. Her book club endorsement of former heroin addict James Frey's *A Million Little Pieces* blew up when it was uncovered that Frey fabricated most of the book. Oprah eventually apologized for the incident.

Cohen is having great fun getting his guests, like Susan Sarandon and Kathy Bates, to talk about pot. Martha Stewart said on the show that she almost asked for a puff off a sloppily rolled joint she'd seen on the way to the studio, and that "of course" she knew how to roll one properly.

Stewart had her eyes opened to the injustices of the drug war when she took a prison rap for the true stock manipulators who bankrupted our country. In her 2005 holiday message from prison, she wrote, "I beseech you all. . . to encourage the American people to ask for reforms, both in sentencing guidelines, in length of incarceration for nonviolent first-time offenders, and for those involved in drug-taking." She and the artist formerly known as Snoop Dogg baked brownies and rapped about the green kind on her show in 2009. "Why not bake 'em at 4 hundred and 20 degrees?" asked Snoop. Stewart is now offering free patterns for her hemp/cotton yarn line.

Photo: Getty Images / Sponsored by www.GreenRushConsulting.com

Sarah Silverman

"God, we were so free."

Comedienne Sarah Silverman won an Emmy in 2014 for writing her variety special *We Are Miracles,* but it was for showing off her vape pen on the red carpet, calling it "liquid marijuana," that she went viral. (Silverman also stood out in her long, green dress on a night when almost every actress wore red.)

Silverman said afterwards she didn't "have a puff-a-roony" until after the event. But kicking off her shoes and speaking about molecules hurtling through space for her speech seemed the Stoniest Awards Show Moment since Whoopi Goldberg accepted her Oscar for *Ghost* (see p. 95).

"It's down to, like, four nights a week," Silverman told *Rolling Stone* in 2005 about her pot habit. "After I perform, I have to have it. I used to like all that stuff, mushrooms, acid. I think I was high from nineteen to twenty-one years old. It was the best time…Finally we got back to my apartment which was painted dark purple to match my bong…God! We were so free."

The episode "High, It's Sarah" from season 2 of her sitcom *The Sarah Silverman Program* had some interesting and unexpected insights about what getting high's all about: wondering if the ideas you have while high are valid, and seeing blatant conspiracies where, it turns out, they do exist.

Silverman talks about marijuana vs. alcohol in her book *Bedwetter* and in 2008 she spoke about her philosophy of marijuana (and everything): "Make it a treat, not a career."

In the intro to *We Are Miracles*, Silverman smokes a joint outside Largo, the L.A. club where it's filmed. She plays a serious role in her latest film, *I Smile Back,* about a housewife battling depression, alcoholism and drug abuse.

Roseanne Barr

"The War on Drugs is a war on poor people."

The gutsiest and most populist comedienne ever, Roseanne Barr has followed her television and film successes with a writing career. Barr's latest book, *Roseannearchy: Dispatches from the Nut Farm* contains more homespun humor from a woman whose rocky road of fame has matured her voice. In it, she explains that her sincere and failed attempt to sing the National Anthem was fueled by psychiatric drugs and a lack of "a natural substance called THC":

"Shortly after the National Anthem horror, I started to feel as though I were waking up from a bad nightmare. The Prozac, Zoloft, Klonopin, and several other mood-altering drugs that had been prescribed for me by psychiatrists (whose destruction by Scientology I now welcome) for my 'Multiple-Personality Bipolar Obsessive-Compulsive Disorder' were no longer doing the trick of shielding me from reality. I became even more depressed than normal, like a lot of people do after they take antidepressants. I had stopped smoking the Herb of the Goddess that had forever kept me balanced enough to become successful and rich, in order to support my then-husband's 'sobriety,' and that led to massive bipolar troubles that were all capped off with tons of psychiatrists and psychiatric drugs, none of which helped with my problems at all and, in fact, made them even worse."

Barr's hilarious 2006 HBO special "Blonde and Bitchin'" contained her trenchant observation, "The War on Drugs is a war on poor people using street drugs waged by rich people on prescription drugs." She repeated the line during a rousing stump speech delivered at Oaksterdam University while running for U.S. President (and Prime Minister of Israel) in 2012. In 2013, Barr joined 174 other prominent women (and men) signing an open letter to Obama calling for an end to the injustice of the war on drugs. Other signatories included Eva Longoria, Margaret Cho, Rosario Dawson, Scarlett Johannson, Demi Moore, three Kardashians (Kim, Khloe and Kourtney), Ani Di Franco, Missy Elliot, Jennifer Hudson, Natalie Maines, Nicki Minaj, Michelle Alexander, and Naomi Klein.

Joan Rivers

"We had fun."

Joan Rivers—a breakthrough artist who was the first comedienne to perform at Carnegie Hall—was also a prolific writer, penning a dozen books, starting with *Having a Baby Can Be A Scream* and the best-selling *The Life and Hard Times of Heidi Abramowitz*.

As self-deprecating as Phyllis Diller before her, Rivers was a favorite of Johnny Carson while telling jokes like, "At 30, a woman is an 'old maid'; at 90, a man is still 'a catch.'" But when Rivers accepted an offer for her own talk show on the Fox network, produced by her husband Edgar, Johnny never spoke to her again. Edgar committed suicide after Joan's show was canceled, leaving her to raise their daughter Melissa alone. She worked wherever she could after that, turning her shrewd eye outwards, and was open about the plastic surgeries she endured to stay viewable.

Rivers won an Emmy for her daytime talk show, and was nominated for Drama Desk and Tony awards for her performance in the title role of *Sally Marr...and Her Escorts*, a 1994 Broadway play based on the life of Lenny Bruce's mother. Later, she won *Celebrity Apprentice*, headed the hilarious *Fashion Police* and did a reality TV show with her daughter Melissa.

It was on her reality show that Rivers smoked pot in 2012. When TMZ asked her who else she'd smoked with back in the day, she replied, "Oh, Betty White, George Carlin, Woody Allen, Bill Cosby. . . we had fun."

"Can we talk?" was Rivers's catch phrase, and she talked up a storm about marijuana on an *Access Live* appearance where she says she loves marijuana "because it makes you giggly," but that she rarely smoked it because "it makes you eat." (Interestingly, a new study says that although females seem more sensitive to marijuana, it's males who most often get the munchies.)

Susan Sarandon

"I would much rather my kids smoke weed than drink, except that it's illegal."

In a 1992 interview about *Light Sleeper*, in which she played a cocaine dealer, actress/activist Susan Sarandon told Robert Scheer of the *Los Angeles Times*, "Cocaine didn't interest me. Not at all. I'm way, way back in the early pot, and mushrooms, organic, not all these chemical things that split you and do horrible things. They're too antisocial... The only thing political about [*Light Sleeper*] is that usually in the films and news, drugs are always connected with people of color. You never see rich, white, upwardly mobile people. In this movie, that's who I, the drug queen, sell to."

On film, Sarandon smokes pot with (and without) Kevin Costner in *Bull Durham*, wherein she muses about philosophy and literature, and concludes, "This world is made for those who aren't cursed with self-awareness." She's seen in *The Witches of Eastwick*, based on the John Updike novel, in which pot smoking takes place with the devilish Jack Nicholson. In *Stepmom* with Julia Roberts, Sarandon's character uses medical marijuana to treat cancer.

"I'm not drinker, I'm more of a stoner," Sarandon recently told the *New York Times*. Inducted among 15 other personalities into the New Jersey Hall of Fame in May 2010, Sarandon said: "We've legalized marijuana recently. Medical marijuana, but the rest will come." (She was right.) She recently told *AARP Magazine*, "I would much rather my kids smoke weed than drink, except that it's illegal."

The torch is passed to a new generation: Eva Amurri Martino, Sarandon's daughter with Italian film director Franco Amurri, appeared in the 2008 film *Middle of Nowhere*, in which she drives a pot dealer around one summer to make money for college. The scene wherein he justifies his career choice is one of the most cogent arguments for legalization ever made.

Cameron Diaz

"We only had two dollars for a joint."

Cameron Diaz, who catapulted to fame in her first movie role opposite Jim Carrey in *Mask*, has been photographed passing a joint to Drew Barrymore and told *GQ* in December 2007 about her life as a weed-smoking surfer in high school: "It took two hours to get (to the beach) on the bus. You stayed all day, ate corn dogs. We had only two dollars for a joint."

Something (everything?) about her made Ben Stiller chase Diaz across the country in *Something About Mary*, and when the characters reconnect they smoke a joint together. On TBS's *Lopez Tonight* promoting her appearance in *Green Hornet* with Seth Rogen, Diaz spoke about being from the LBC (Long Beach) where she "had to have" bought weed from Snoop Dogg. "So you were green even in high school?" asked host George Lopez. "Oh yeah," she replied.

Diaz was surprisingly convincing as a dowdy housewife in *Being John Malkovich*. In it, her character Lottie convinces her husband Craig (John Cusak) to invite the object of both their desires, Maxine (Catherine Keener) to dinner. "It will be fine, we'll smoke a joint," she counters when Craig mounts an excuse. After dinner, Maxine rolls a joint for her admirers. It just gets wilder from there.

Diaz carried the movie *Bad Teacher* in a rare comedic starring role for a woman. Rather than the usual lowbrow fare, the film has heart and soul, sort of a *Private Benjamin* meets *School of Rock*, complete with a terrific performance by Phyllis Smith (*The Office*) smoking a doobie.

Casting her then–boy toy Justin Timberlake as a nerdy pants-wetter who parodies himself singing a love song in pitch-perfect style, Diaz transcends the harkened-to Edward James Olmos and Michelle Pfeiffer as cool teachers who find their humanity in tragedy. *Bad Teacher*, like Cameron Diaz, handles marijuana in perfect irony, moderation, and jubilation. She received her sixth ALMA Award nomination for the performance. *Bad Teacher 2* has been announced.

Photo: Daniel Roos

Barbara Ehrenreich

"The engaging qualities I believe I have to offer...can all be trumped by my pee."

For her book *Nickel and Dimed: On (Not) Getting By in America*, author and NORML board member Barbara Ehrenreich took a series of minimum-wage jobs, and wrote about facing pre-employment drug testing knowing that she had marijuana in her system. "It rankles at some deep personal, physical level to know that the many engaging qualities I believe I have to offer—friendliness, reliability, willingness to learn—can all be trumped by my pee."

She went deeper into the economic injustice of the situation, writing, "Corporate decision makers, and even some two-bit entrepreneurs like my boss at The Maids, occupy an economic position miles above that of the underpaid people whose labor they depend on. For reasons that have more to do with class—and often racial—prejudice than with actual experience, they tend to fear and distrust the category of people from which they recruit their workers. Hence the perceived need for repressive management and intrusive measures like drug and personality testing."

Ehrenreich's *Witches, Midwives, & Nurses: A History of Women Healers* is essential reading on the subject, to be followed by *For Her Own Good: Two Centuries of the Experts Advice to Women* and *The Hearts of Men: American Dreams and the Flight from Commitment*. With her usual unerring logic and clarity, she took on the pinking of breast cancer in in her article "Welcome to Cancerland," and addressed our obsession with positive thinking in *Bright Sided*. Her book about ancient ecstatic rites *Dancing in the Streets: A History of Collective Joy*, is fascinating.

In her latest work, *Living with a Wild God*, the famous scientist, atheist and feminist describes mystical experiences she had in her adolescence, following a rigorous study of religion and philosophy. When asked by the *New York Times* magazine, "Imagine a 14-year-old you living in the present day having visions like that. What do you think would happen to her?" her reply was, "Oh, I think she'd be given a lot of drugs today."

Photo: Susana Millman   www.mamarazi.com

Carolyn Garcia

"It has now become like the wine or brandy industry."

Carolyn Garcia, the first wife of Grateful Dead guitarist Jerry Garcia, was nicknamed "Mountain Girl" by one of Ken Kesey's Merry Pranksters, and it's fitting: she's as strong and solid as a mountain. When Kesey was arrested for pot in 1965, she openly told news reporters, "I'm not weeping with remorse."

Soon afterwards, she was gifted with four marijuana seeds brought back from Vietnam by a veteran, and grew them so well that the resulting buds were considered too strong. Trained in science and interested in the then-unknown field of organic gardening, she began growing several other cannabis strains from seed, again doing so well that she was inundated with requests to share her secrets. She decided to write what became a seminal book on marijuana cultivation, *Primo Plant: Growing Sinsemilla Marijuana*, first published in 1976. The book quickly became a bestseller, selling 50,000 copies in two years' time and helping to start the trend of growing quality home-grown sinsemilla among the back-to-the-landers of her generation.

Garcia joined the board of the Dead's Rex Foundation around 1990 during Redwood Summer, and helped direct funding to groups protecting ancient forests in Mendocino County, California, as well as to the Innocence Project, Mercy Corps, and many others. She serves on the advisory board to the Marijuana Policy Project, and helped shape the Women's Visionary Council, a group that holds events across the country to highlight women's research in entheogenics. She has also raised three daughters.

"I was definitely a seeker...I would question every single thing. That was sort of my style," Garcia told an interviewer in 1997. She embraces the movement towards a broader spectrum of cultivars containing THC and/or CBD. "It has now become like the wine or brandy industry," she told www.hemp.org in 2014. "There are a lot of very hip, smart, thoughtful people who have gotten into the production."

Rita Marley

"I have my one draw occasionally."

Born to a musical family in Jamaica, Alpharita "Rita" Anderson began singing at weddings at an early age, and later sang lead in her girl group The Soulettes, known as "the Supremes of the Caribbean." At the age of 19, she married Bob Marley and had four children with him, as well as helping to raise several of the children he had with other women. Along with Marcia Griffiths and Judy Mowatt, Rita formed the I Threes and sang backup for Bob on the tours that brought reggae music to the world.

When Rita first began to embrace Rastafarianism and ganja smoking, neither were well accepted in Jamaica. "My Aunty began to worry, my God, is Rita smoking hat stuff, that terrible stuff that would make you go crazy and put you in prison," Rita wrote in her autobiography *No Woman No Cry*. "I *had* started smoking a little herb....I liked smoking for the way it made me feel—cooled out and meditative...."

After meeting with Rasta elders, she writes, "The whole thing seemed intelligent to me; it wasn't just about smoking herb, it was more a philosophy that carried a history with it. That's what really pulled my interest, the powerful history that hadn't been taught to me in school."

Rita's 1981 hit "One Draw" was controversial because it was set in a school. In March 2014, she released "One Draw" for the first time in a digital format, saying, "Marijuana is a herb which helps produce the serenity and insight, it is a healing herb when used properly.... I support legislation of Marijuana, as Marijuana in its natural form is one of the safest therapeutically active substances known to mankind and I know this because I have my one draw occasionally."

Upon the announcement of worldwide cannabis brand Marley Natural in November 2014, Rita said, "My husband believed 'the herb' was a natural and positive part of life, and he felt it was important to the world. He looked forward to this day."

Photo by Bruce Comer Jr.

Kacey Musgraves
"Follow Your Arrow"

Singer/songwriter Kacey Musgraves picked up two Grammys in 2014 and performed Brandy Clark's song "Follow Your Arrow" on the award show, with the lyric:

So make lots of noise
Kiss lots of boys
Or kiss lots of girls
If that's something you're into
When the straight and narrow
Gets a little too straight
Roll up a joint—or don't (I would)
Just follow your arrow
Wherever it points

Musgraves looks a lot more like Princess Kate than a stereotypical pothead. The video for "Follow Your Arrow" features the singer in Daisy Duke shorts, a cowboy hat and toy guns, reminiscent of the act of Tokin' Woman Candy Barr. Like Tokin' Woman Besse Smith on her 1937 recording of "Gimmie a Pigfoot," Musgraves waits until the last verse to add her own reefer admission. She sang it with the "I would" on the Grammys broadcast.

In March 2013 the *Hollywood Reporter* called Musgraves "The Weed-Smoking, Ball-Busting, Girl-Kissing Country Singer," and reported that in 2011, she "was doing sit-down acoustic gigs" playing songs with lyrics like, 'My idea of heaven is to burn one with John Prine.'" (The first song on the first John Prine album is "Illegal Smile.")

Musgraves performed "Follow Your Arrow" at a UMG luncheon for hundreds of country radio programmers in Nashville. "Afterward, the radio types were all abuzz about what a brilliantly catchy and clever ditty it was… and how they could never play it on their stations," the *Reporter* wrote. It was the lowest-charting record to ever win song of the year at the CMA Awards.

Photo: Getty Images / Sponsored by Liana Limited www.lianaltd.com

Miley Cyrus

"I think alcohol is way more dangerous than marijuana."

How can a girl get attention these days in the media meatgrinder that *Penthouse* once depicted on its cover? When a young woman has to resort to riding and licking construction equipment in the nude so that we'll listen to her song, it's our society that's really reached a new low.

You can't blame Cyrus for needing to compete with the hired nude girls in Robin Thicke's idiotic "Blurred Lines" video, and you gotta admit she came in like a wrecking, twerking ball to take Thicke out, even casting him as a female dwarf in her performance at the 2013 European MTV awards in Amsterdam.

To cap it off, after winning "Best Video" for "Wrecking Ball," Cyrus pulled a joint out of a Chanel bag and lit it onstage—and no one was talking about anything else, even after the U.S. censored the event in a nonsmoking version.

Cyrus's blunt move out-doobed Lady Gaga, who smoked a giant joint onstage at her concert in Amsterdam in 2012, saying, "It has totally changed my life and I've really cut down on drinking. It has been a totally spiritual experience for me with my music." Soon afterwards, Gaga labeled herself as addicted to pot, but then said it made her feel like she was 17 again (which doesn't sound so awful).

Filmed in 2010 but not released until 2012, Cyrus's movie *LOL* has an rather interesting take on marijuana, with highschoolers and parents all toking up. *LOL* saw limited release but would have done better had Cyrus toked herself in the film, and it was released the year it was made, when she was in the news for smoking "salvia."

Cyrus hosted the 2015 MTV awards and held an unlit joint onstage while dressed as a rainbow flag. Backstage after the show, she lit the joint and passed it to reporters. Her new song "Dooo It" has the sweet lyrics, "I feel like I am one with the universe…Yo, sing about love, love is what you need / Loving what you sing, and loving smoking weed."

Charlo Greene

"I will be fighting for freedom and fairness."

As Scoop Nisker said, "If you don't like the news, go out and make some of it yourself." News reporter and Alaska Cannabis Club owner Charlo Greene did just that in September 2015 when she quit her job on the air so that she could spend her time campaigning for Measure 2, to legalize marijuana in Alaska.

"Instead of standing on the sidelines and talking about it as a reporter, I will be fighting for freedom and fairness in Alaska," Greene said. Her move inspired people to write in applauding her courage and saying, "I am registering to vote; let's go and do this. I'm behind you."

Greene's campaign was able to make news of the fact that although voters had approved medical marijuana in Alaska in 1998, no dispensaries had been permitted in the state. She highlighted the relative harmfulness of alcohol compared to marijuana, using her own experience as an example. Greene told *Vice* magazine that she, like many Alaskans, drank excessively while in high school, but that she consciously switched to cannabis. "I went from failing an entire semester, to the next semester, and every semester after that, being on the Dean's List. I graduated *cum laude*. And that's because I was smoking weed! I sat my ass at home and did what I needed to do, and I never woke up with a hangover because of it, or got behind the wheel and ran over a family or anything because of it."

"You struck a nerve with the community," Snoop Dogg told her in an interview with his GGN network. "You show that it's not just a bunch of thug dudes that's trying to push weed, but it's women and they speak with intelligence and speak from a right frame of mind." Snoop pledged to go to Alaska and perform if Measure 2 prevailed.

"Yes, I smoke weed," says Greene. "And yes, I'm still a contributing member of society...I'm not going to apologize for the choices I've made. It's time to end prohibition on a global scale."

Index

9 to 5 107, 109
Alice in Wonderland 75
Alcott, Louisa May 28-29
Angelou, Maya 88-89
Aniston, Jennifer 92-93
Anslinger, Harry J. 57
Anthony, Susan B. 45
Asterion plant 11
Baal/Bel 15
Baker, Josephine 50-51
Bankhead, Tallulah 47, 60-61
Barr, Candy 70-71, 129
Barr, Roseanne 114-115
Bates, Kathy 111
Beauvoir, Simone de 66-67
Bell, Gertrude 39, 40-41
Benet, Sula 11
Bewitched 45
Bingen, Hildegarde von 20-21
Blackmore, Susan 98-99
Blavatsky, Helena 34-35, 37
Bowles, Paul 39, 45, 101
Cho, Margaret 115
Circe 13
Clare, Ada 26-27
Clark, Brandy 105, 129
Clinton, Hillary 103
Collins, Joan 71
Crosby, David 79, 81
Cyrus, Miley 130-131
Dawson, Rosario 115
Delphic oracle 13
Demeter 13
Diaz, Cameron 120-121
Dinesen, Isak 52-53
Dionysus 13, 85
drug testing 123
Di Franco, Ani 115

Earlywine, Mitch 1
Eberhardt, Isabelle 38-39, 101
Ehrenreich, Barbara 122-123
Eleusis 13
Eliot, George 24-25
Elliot, Cass 78-79
Elliot, Missy 115
Emerson, Ralph Waldo 25
Etheridge, Melissa 104-105
Fawcett, Farrah 71
Finn, Elisabeth 23
Fisher, Carrie 85
Fitzgerald, Ella 63, 65
Fonda, Jane 107, 108-109
Frogs, The 11, 13
Gaga, Lady 131
Garcia, Carolyn 124-125
Gilgamesh 5
Goldberg, Whoopi 94-95, 113
Goodman, Benny 55, 59
Gonne, Maud 36-37
Greene, Charlo 132-133
Hathsheput 9, 11
Helen of Troy 12-13
Hera 11
Hellman, Lillian 109
hemp 9, 18, 19, 32, 33
Herodotus 7, 13
Holiday, Billie 56-57, 65
Huxley, Aldous 49, 53
Hynde, Chrissie 96-97
Ishtar 4-5, 15
Jezebel 14-15, 65
Johannson, Scarlett 115
John, Augustus 47, 49
Joplin, Janis 76-77, 87
kaneh bosm 11, 17
Kardashians 115

Kidman, Nicole 41
Krupa, Gene 59, 65
lang, k.d. 79
Laurençin, Marie 42-43
Lawford, Christopher 85
Leeds, Lila 68-69
Lincoln, Mary Todd 32-33
Longoria, Eva 115
Lotus eaters 13, 29
Ludlow, Fitz Hugh 27
Magu 18-19
Maher, Bill 83
Marley, Rita 126-127
Martin, Bijou 61
Martineau, Harriet 23
McCartney, Linda 86-87
McGovern, George 79, 81
Mead, Margaret 72-73
Mengers, Sue 82-83
Midler, Bette 83
Mitchum, Robert 69
Moby Dick 15
Moore, Demi 115
Moorhead, Agnes 45
Murat, Violette 43, 46-47
Musgraves, Kacey 128-129
nepenthe 13
O'Day, Anita 64-65
Odyssey, The 13
Palin, Sarah 103-104
Parvati 16-17
Phillips, Michelle 79
Picasso, Pablo 43
Polosmak, Natalia 7
Princess Kate 31, 129
Princess Ukok 6-7
Queen Latifah 55
Queen of Heaven 5, 15
Queen Victoria 30-31

Reiner, Erica 5
Reynolds, John Russell 30, 31
Rigoglioso, Marguerite 11, 13
Rivers, Joan 116-117
Roberts, Julia 119
Rogen, Seth 81, 121
Rogers, Mary Eliza 23
Ross, Annie 63
Sarandon, Susan 25, 118-119
Seshat 8-9, 11
Shaw, Dora 27
Sheba, Queen of 10-11, 101
Shiva 16-17
Silkwood, Karen 90-91
Silverman, Sarah 112-113
Slick, Grace 74-75
Smith, Bessie 54-55, 77
Smith, Patti 39, 100-101
Snoop Dogg 111, 121
Solomon 11, 101
Stanhope, Lucy 23
Stein, Gertrude 43, 44-45, 79, 83
Stevens Case, Marie 27
Stewart, Martha 111
Streep, Meryl 53, 91
Streisand, Barbra 80-81, 83
Swanson, Gloria 77
Taylor, Elizabeth 77, 84-85
Taylor-Young, Leigh 45
Toklas, Alice B. 44-45
Tomlin, Lily 106-107
Tree, Iris 47, 48-49
Vaughan, Sarah 62-63
White, Betty 117
Williams, Mary Lou 58-59
Winfrey, Oprah 120-111
Women of Algiers 22
Yeats, William Butler 37
Zoroaster 15

Acknowledgements

The author would like to thank the
following sponsors for photos in this book:

Liana Limited www.LianaLtd.com
Green Rush Consulting www.GreenRushConsulting.com
Paradigm Cannabis Group www.ParadigmCannabis.com
Giggle Therapeutics www.GiggleTherapeutics.com
Green Flash Glass www.GreenFlashGlass.com
Michelle and Michael Aldrich
LaTanya Linzie
Kyndra Miller

Interested sponsors for more Tokin' Women
in future editions can contact the publisher.

Tokin' Women is dedicated to the women presented here,
and to activists everywhere who work to free the holy, healing herb.

Special thanks to Dale Gieringer of California NORML,
Michael & Cindy Horowitz of Flashback Books, and Michael &
Michelle Aldrich for generously sharing their love of learning with me.
To Mark Weiman of Regent Press for expert advice and assistance, and
to Jackie Gay Wilson for her excellent proofreading and copyediting.
To so many others who have encouraged this work and offered ideas,
among them Anne Marie Kirkpatrick, DeeDee Kirkwood, Lajuana
Latiolais, Denise Martellacci, Debby Goldsberry and Sarah Cross.
To biographers, librarians and book store owners everywhere,
especially in Humboldt county and Berkeley, California,
where I uncovered many of the stories in this book.
And to my family & friends for their love and support.

Coming Soon from Evangelista Sista Press

The Trimmer's Handbook

Full of practical advice and pointers on everything from legal considerations and social interactions to which brand of scissors to use, this handy book provides useful information for would-be trimmers and the farmers who employ them.

Emily Dickinson's Divine Intoxication

A great many of the poems that Emily Dickinson wrote have ecstatic themes. Drawing from her poems and letters, and her herbarium, this book makes a bold case for hidden reasons behind Dickinson's daily devotion to consciousness exploration.

Confessions of the Happy Hempstress

A rollicking ride through the early days of the hemp movement, this memoir details encounters with movement figures like Jack Herer and Tommy Chong, and other famous folk the author met while she pursued her calling and cause.

Evangelista Sista Press, an imprint of Regent Press
www.RegentPress.net

www.ingramcontent.com/pod-product-compliance
Lightning Source LLC
Chambersburg PA
CBHW061220070526
44584CB00029B/3916